THIS BOOK

was created with the generous spirit and assistance
of our sponsors who share a passionate
commitment to help tell the story of
how we became Americans
400 years ago.

DOMINION

ROBERT H. AND CLARICE SMITH

EXXONMOBIL

TED AND SHEILA WESCHLER

THE HOOK

VIRGINIA FOUNDATION FOR THE HUMANITIES

VIRGINIA NATIONAL BANK

EMBARQ

EMPIRES

IN THE FOREST

JAMESTOWN AND THE BEGINNING OF AMERICA

WORDS AVERY CHENOWETH

PHOTOGRAPHS ROBERT LLEWELLYN

INTRODUCTION

by former Virginia Governor Mark R. Warner

Empires in the Forest opens on a wise note: No story really begins where you think it does.

That's especially true in a young place like America.

Consider the stories of people. When the English sailors disembarked from the *Susan Constant*, the *Godspeed*, and the *Discovery* on the banks of the river they named for King James I, they found a thriving society among the Algonquian-speaking farming people—tribes that had been telling their stories in North America for more than 10,000 years and in the land along Chesapeake Bay for at least 300.

Or the stories of history. Many remember the *Mayflower*'s arrival as this country's beginning, but the new residents of Jamestown had already been writing the American story for more than thirteen years in Virginia when that ship sailed into Massachusetts Bay.

Or the story of captivity. When the House of Burgesses first met in July 1619, it introduced a basic tenet of freedom to the colonies—the institution of self-government. But one month later, a Dutch man o' war introduced the evil institution of slavery when it deposited twenty African captives on Jamestown's shores.

Or the story of politics. History's greatest experiment in democracy was born when the British colonies declared independence, but the seeds of the story of self-governance were planted more than 500 years before on a field at Runnymeade, to say nothing of the forum of Athens 1,500 years before that.

Or the story of ideas. Virginians rightly regard Jefferson as America's greatest thinker, but other great minds told the story of democracy and freedom decades before Jefferson declared those truths to be self-evident.

Or the story of equality. The Supreme Court made American education truly public in 1954, but the story of its decision was already underway when a young Oliver Hill entered law school more than twenty years before, pledging to "go out and fight segregation."

Or the story of the land itself. While the settlers saw Jamestown's deep water as a haven to protect themselves from potential Spanish attackers, their settlement marked yet another chapter in the ongoing story of rivalry between warring European nations.

Each of these seminal stories points to an equally decisive story years before—or at least that's what we think today. We're always looking for new ways to help us understand where we've been. Our past doesn't change, but our understanding of it is constantly evolving.

History books once told stories that started with Jamestown's settlers and ignored the people they met when they arrived. What will tomorrow's history say?

The answers change, but the questions remain constant. Who were the people that came here? Who was here before that? How did they get here?

4

Why did they stop here? Why did they stay?

We'll probably always be seeking the earliest answers to these questions, and we'll never fully understand what came before.

But we do know that a new chapter in human history started at Jamestown. When the British settlers came ashore, they found an abundance of fruit and flowers like they had never imagined. They found water and land that would shape the story of Virginia's future.

As the settlement became the colony, and the colony became the Commonwealth, each generation of new Americans found among Virginia's geography a place to write its own chapter.

Jefferson wrote just one book, and he devoted nearly the first half of *Notes on the State of Virginia* to describing the Commonwealth's "Boundaries; Rivers; Sea-ports; Mountains; Cascades; Productions Mineral, Vegetable, and Animal; and Climate" before he first mentioned people, let alone the political arts to which he devoted so much of his life. He described a land that constantly called him home from a lifetime of travel around the world. That same land remains a beacon today.

Today, people from around the world call Virginia home. In one Virginia school system alone, students hail from more than 150 countries—nearly every country in the world—and speak more than 100 languages as their first tongue. They and their families have been drawn to Virginia by the same hopes and the same appeal that have drawn generations of new Virginians.

The draw of Virginia is deep. It's a force that Avery Chenoweth and Robert Lllewellyn capture with eloquence and beauty.

Their images in words and photographs recall the century-old words of a Virginia guidebook published at Jamestown's 1907 tercentenary: "The Far East has its Mecca, Palestine its Jerusalem, France its Lourdes, and Italy its Loretto, but America's only shrines are her altars of patriotism—the first and most potent being Jamestown; the sire of Virginia, and Virginia the mother of this great Republic."

Why should anyone read the story of Jamestown and the tale of Virginia?

After all, depending on which numbers you accept, the 400 years of American history that began at Jamestown probably constitute no more than 0.0002% of human history.

We'll surely be debating this question at least another 400 years. The answers will surely change at least 400 times as well, because in a place as young as America, even the oldest stories are just getting started.

Perhaps Patrick Henry, Virginia's first elected Governor, said it best: "I have but one lamp by which my feet are guided, and that is the lamp of experience. I know no way of judging of the future but by the past."

The tale we tell today is the American story, born in 1607 at Jamestown. Four centuries later, it's reborn every day, in Virginia. ∎

PREFACE

All of us saw the wall of cloud across the water, and felt the ship falling and rising in our legs. A few days earlier, the replica *Susan Constant* had sailed out of the Jamestown Settlement into the Chesapeake Bay. Two days of August sunshine had left the small crew of forty-some men, three women, and a few boys dry and drowsy with routine. The morning had passed with figures posing high in the riggings, or in profile against the sky. The humidity of afternoon had deepened and a light rain was falling. Water and cloud now formed a dimensionless mass of dark that spread across the bay, lit with threads of red lightning.

We had come to the bay to find an elusive slip of meaning from the Jamestown colony—the first permanent English colony in America—and to see what insights we could nudge loose from its history. After more than four centuries, the famous people of the Jamestown story have become American legends. They inspire books and movies, myth and entertainment. But they were people first, humane and inhumane, torn with conflict. Those were the people whom Bob and I tried to find and understand. *Empires in the Forest* is our attempt to present them as living individuals in their moment, an endeavor to take the reader on a journey in time and empathy, to the edge of history where America began—and then back, with a new perspective on how American Identity became what it is today. Sometimes, to understand the dead, you have to go near them.

The captain's eyes cut to one side; the radio was announcing an alert: seven waterspouts were whipping ahead in the dark. Faces round, thin, youthful, and bearded formed a group portrait. They were volunteers, not sailors. Their costumes were damp, glasses wet; chop splashed; and no one heard the light slap of ropes in the wind. The captain ordered us below.

Below decks we bent forward into the kind of narrow space that John Smith, John Rolfe, and others had known four hundred years ago. The air was close, the ceiling no more than a few feet overhead as we lay among coils of rope in the dim. Fresh air surged in through a porthole. The ship slowed, its engines now rumbling, but we felt it—the ship balancing round an invisible axis. With roll, the sides swerved up; with pitch, the boat nosed down and up. All was well. But then there was yaw: the nose twisted right, the tail went left, pitch and roll came in on the chorus, and your senses swung loose in the hammock of your brain. In the obscurity, bodies lay on their backs, doped with medicine, panting for air in the ninety-degree heat. And we were only on four-foot swells on the Chesapeake—leaving it impossible to imagine being aboard this boat on the Atlantic, in twenty-foot seas harassed by a hurricane, crammed in with 150 people, livestock, and water exploding in.

Imagine we must, though. History is always in motion. Even as we sail forward, its deep, oceanic current moves us ceaselessly into the past. In this book we imagine all the things that were in motion in Virginia four centuries ago, a story that is experimental. While scholars provide facts and dates, and journals conspiracies and temperaments, the interior lives of the Powhatan and English will always remain mysterious. We make an anachronistic fallacy if we imagine that we can answer what they really felt, emotions as tantalizing yet as inconclusive as those felt one day on a re-created ship.

My own comfort with the history was formal—and as polite as sitting in church. Pocahontas had loved John Smith, but married John Rolfe—but was that before or after the Puritans? That was a children's story, without meaning or relevance to anyone in America today. Sometime in my early youth, a period beginning with Indian Guides and ending with a visit to the Trail of Tears museum in North Carolina, the story of the Indians made an unbearable impression—they were gone and what had happened was a tragedy that could not be fixed by crying in the car. Yet what we found on our quest around Virginia will come as news to only the unenlightened, like myself: the Indians of Virginia, the Powhatans, are not gone but staunchly here. The story we found was that of resiliency and tenacity, but also of something more. We found an almost ineffable metaphysics of identity, in which myth and memory coalesce in the prism of landscape; and to neglect this dynamic is to risk losing not only who we are, but also, perhaps, the medium in which we form a humane society. In the end, our quest became to know who we are as Americans.

And so we began by going forward into the internecine dark of what went on between the Powhatan, English, and Africans, and the ameliorations of a few historic people. Though we can never know them, of course, this book is about the rise of an American Identity from a suite of social behaviors, personal and communal, the wind in history's sails. We cannot feel this in a museum, and might as well take this framework out of the harbor.

We may have smoothed in to port at dusk that day, but we had experienced a few moments out of ourselves on the storming waters of the bay. Around us vessels of endless design and media bear us through the void toward others, by print, stone, story or other craft. While we all have assumptions about what happened; much of it cannot be known, and what follows in these pages are my assumptions along with fictional elisions. The sole intent is to *be* with them for a while. To imagine the lives of those who died 400 years ago is to reawaken an essential empathy for others.

If we suspend our notions, we may experience a similar levitation—an older sensation of the bay and the sky, the heat and dark of the storm, the desire and disquiet of some remarkable people. Their lives became legends and gave shape to our own. In aspiring to know them intimately, we honor their memory. ▪

THEY SAILED SOUTH UNTIL "THE BUTTER MELTED" AND THEN TURNED RIGHT, THE

COMMON DIRECTIONS GIVEN THEN FOR SAILING TO THE CANARIES. FROM THOSE ISLANDS THEY THEN

LAUNCHED OUT AGAIN AND CROSS THE OCEAN SEA

NEWLY CHRISTENED THE ATLANTIC.

No story really begins where you think it does.

Although many people mistakenly assume colonial America began in New England, an older and richer story lies under the woods and meadows of Virginia. Here, in a century of invasion and mayhem, native and foreign peoples clashed, and in resolving the crisis many of them became the alloy we call American. Yet, the people who once walked these woods and swam these rivers are now overshadowed with myth and entertainment, obscuring their lives and even the landscape in which they lived so fiercely. Caveats apply to the pages that follow, but if we model some psychology on the bones of their stories—building with oral and written accounts, and sculpting with judicious imagination—we might reanimate their eyes and faces, and learn how we share their conflicts not only as Americans but also as individuals in our own private searching.

In the lives of people who died four centuries ago we might understand more of who we are as a nation, where we have been and where we are going. While we stroll a bit in search of a beginning, we might look back millions of years ago to a time when almost every living thing in Virginia was killed. For what happened in the immemorial past would affect those around Jamestown and shape the rise of an American identity—and this fragment was a piece of the creation.

One evening long ago,

before humans stood up in the African savanna, a star of ice fell into the ocean off the coast of modern Virginia. This dirty snowball had been traveling for so many eons that it was likely flung out of the big bang itself. That afternoon millions of animals in the forest may have felt uneasy and restless, reacting to an odd sensation even as animals do now when they sense an approaching tsunami or some other impending disaster. All they would have seen was the weary pallor of the summer afternoon, humid with carbon dioxide and thick with salt—that, and a dim point of light.

The ocean was wide and shallow; it washed over the palm-shaded beaches of a range that we call the Blue Ridge. Now low, gently rounded shoulders, these mountains then towered, vaulting and steep, luminous with a rain forest raucous with harlequin birds. Rodents nipped about. Bats hung in batches. The dawn horse, no larger than a suburban Labrador, cantered on its toes, and not far away stood the impervious uintatherium, a kind of rhinoceros, its head studded with tusks. This was another hour in the moist Eocene, the age of mammals. At a distance of some thirty-five million years, this era is so otherworldly, from its atmosphere to its geology and everything in between, that what happened next could have occurred on another planet—beneath another sun and other stars.

The forest stilled. A band of tiny apes stopped chatting and eating and looked up, their eyes blinking amid the leaves—the low star over the ocean was growing larger and larger.

Then it hit. The sky split. Fire scored the atmosphere and the horizon went white. The ocean vaporized. Water rising hundreds of feet raced out from the explosion. The forest burst into flame. The shock wave killed millions of animals; the tsunami crashed into the Blue Ridge. The meteor, two miles in width, excavated a crater fifty miles across and a mile deep. The ocean raced back and silted in the crater with the centuries. Almost all evidence of the cataclysm slowly vanished. All that can be seen of it today is a few faint ridgelines and a body of water that we call the Chesapeake Bay.

Not all evidence of the explosion slid under the ocean and silt. For almost 1,000 miles all around the site of the crash, the sky sizzled, though not with rain. Hot sand blown from the blast soared into the atmosphere like the ash and rock of a volcano, and fell, cooling on its way down. Beads of glass lit the sky. The umbrella of tracers shone all the way south to modern Georgia. Molten and amber in color, millions of these shards fired into ocean, river, and forest, only washing up in the slow exfoliations of earth. Millions of years later, when people roamed the land they would sometimes find these little spheres gleaming amid the leaves, decay, and seashells covering the floor of a woodland forest…and they would wear these jewels in their necklaces.

The unknown people who first came to populate this land of creek and wood, meadow and marsh were born to a culture almost without measure. They arrived on a terrain somber with arctic storms, ice, and mammoths; they pursued a life that cannot really be appreciated across a span of more than 10,000 years, if not longer—an elusive continuity going forward into the dark and curving out, at last, under the shadow of European sails.

This cradle of humanity was theirs. These Paleo-Indians came as nomads, arriving on the mountains and looking out upon the plain of meteor hills, there on the waning cusp of the Ice Age. Alpine flowers colored the wind; mountainsides splashed with ice melt; herds of mastodons grazed on thickets of tough grasses; and wolves hunted the length of this warming tundra. These early people fanned out across the plains as far as the ocean, sustaining

13

themselves on the land's bounty.

The climate warmed further; the ocean pushed in over the continental shelf and began flooding the long dry canyon and river of the Chesapeake blast site. More bands of people followed the hunting into the region, and language groups of the contact era—Siouan, Iroquoian, and Algonquian—speak of western and northern origins. Their tools and weapons, like the Clovis point, were big, intended for big animals— beavers seven feet long, sloths twenty- feet tall. The inundation

of warmth in the atmosphere grew an enormous world, and a communicative new brilliance filled the heights and avenues of the conifer forest that covered Virginia. Landscape was more than a home, however; in some smooth elision over time, an early metaphysics of identity flowed into being, in which light and landscape led them into a sense of the divine. In the past, as nomads, divinity had been an abstraction, but now divinity would arise from this place and reflect their identity as they made the land into a place of eloquence—a landscape.

These prehistoric people fled the rising ocean, moved inland, and settled along the rivers. They established hamlets and villages and, for many thousands of years, they continued an ancient pattern of migration, writing in the lines of forest trails the prose of their existence. Their territory would fall into an outline delineated by the animals and the seasons. As the herds of moose, elk, and deer would move, so they would as well. Each base camp supplied them with water and quartz, and a running line of intersection with the herd. The rivers, dropping from the mountains in the sunset, were fresh but fed as well by the ocean

on the sunrise. The estuaries fed them oysters and fish. They used long nets woven of reeds and let the current send a basket of dinner into the traps. Walnuts nestled in green orbs littered the forest floor. Multitudes of berries, red and blue, brightened the hands that gathered them. The fluency and abundance, fresh and at hand, were seen not as incidental—but as providential. These people looked at the world and saw the maker's hand.

He lived in the sky. He was their father and his name was Ahone, the god who had made the earth and the moon and the stars as his companions. (Incidentally, if we consider that an outside force created the Indian world along the tidewater, a curious coincidence appears: from a certain altitude, the site of the meteor strike spreads out across Virginia in the shape of an alien handprint. The withered impression of four fingers, a palm, and a thumb look like a birth-slap in the sand.) Ahone oversaw life among the Indians in a peaceable way. While lesser gods sometimes demanded homage and sacrifice, he was content to let his people thrive without taxing them with demands for food or blood. And yet, like many sky gods around the world, Ahone became remote. He withdrew into the heavens, and did not further involve himself with his creation.

Their Mother God lived with Ahone. Both gods were somewhere out of sight if not out of perception, hovering in a peripheral field of awareness. She fell to earth and was the Corn Mother. Ahone created the world and gave it to the people, as a kind of architect; the Corn Mother fed them with the miraculous plant bearing her name, which they had imported from trade routes south. The runty little plant of ancient Mexico had so thoroughly

flourished under human hands that when it reached the Chesapeake region, it was already a robust crop. It was a miracle plant in a surprising new way: after people learned to cultivate it into a more substantive plant, it in turn reciprocated and cultivated a few gardens into an agricultural district, farmers into traders, villages into towns, and portable huts into permanent buildings. Corn had grown the Aztec into a vast empire, and its arrival on this coast was a harbinger of the societies that might have arisen here one day had the English not arrived.

As distantly as 900 years ago, perhaps, people here grew corn in four rotations from early spring to late fall, producing a cascading cornucopia that they housed in granaries. They interspersed beans and squash along the rows of corn. The unity of the crops prompted the people to call them the Three Sisters. In that name, you can hear a meaningful echo. The three plants together developed complex ecological relationships, drawing and giving strength to one another, much as the women who grew and harvested the crops wove bands of work into social networks that sustained the tribe. In this nearly silent acknowledgment of naming, we can hear faint praise of all the women who nourished their world but whose stories go unheard in the din made by men and war.

Like the Mississippians before them, whose empire covered most of the American South, the women here were not growing crops alone. Agriculture planted new ways of relating to nature and one another; the deeper roots were those of a singular and bonded identity within a location and with the gods who made it, allowing for an

emerging psychology and spirituality of the individual. In a culture in which the women taught girls how to plant, grow, and gather, the women also invariably emphasized the art of discernment—deciding which of the many is best. During a time of change, such a skill might swing away from its accepted uses and challenge the group assessment. The person defying the established customs may feel pressured to lapse back into communal acceptance, or choose to go forward alone, and into a new sense of individualism. Such a path may begin quietly for a child working beside her mother among the rows of corn.

More than merely practical, though, agriculture was also spiritual. Displays of excellence, whether in human skill or flourishing plant, were seen as encounters with *manitu*. This force of life would reveal itself to the witness through an epiphany of spirit, its excellence, and therefore of Ahone. Spirits from this divine energy field would alight and guide an individual and a community. For those who succeeded, their *manitu* was present, but for those who failed, their *manitu* had abandoned them. To pursue life in proper balance could ensure success, but to overreach for that which was outside that balance could mean failure. In 1607, the year the English arrived, the Powhatan were enjoying a rising success.

As spirit imbued the community, *manitu* also inspired individuals. Upon entering puberty, a girl or boy would be blessed by the personal interest of a spirit, or *manit*, who would visit them in a dream, and from then on guide the child down a singular path in pursuit of what we would call destiny. These aspects of life, culture, and individuality were an indivisible unity. For a girl working beside her mother, her life, her discernment, her destiny, her art of growing a self and a community, all flowed freely into her from a world of spirit, material and divine.

Divine hands, inspired yet practical,

seeded their identity into the ground, cultivated this force into communities, and slowed the routine of seasonal migration with the deer herds. A sense of place literally engendered a sense of identity. The people settled, giving up their nomadic ways, gradually changing from hunter-gatherers to farmers. Their numbers grew, as did the complexity of their identity, which they cultivated within the natural and divine spheres. Over the centuries, from the Late Archaic into the Woodlands period—demarcations that follow in Western style the linear evolution of their tools—the peoples of Virginia began to separate out into the names we know them by today. By the seventeenth century, there may have been as many as fifty or sixty tribes living in the Chesapeake Bay area, but only the one known to the English as the Powhatan takes center stage in the Jamestown story. This tribe had been living near the bay for some 300 years.

The Powhatan were led by Wahunsunacock, the tribe's paramount chief, and one of the first leaders in Native American history to stand up to foreign invasion. Overlord of six tribes, he set a course to build a coalition of tribes many times that number. He would make war or negotiate, do anything, to gather other tribes and their estates into his burgeoning chiefdom, which he ruled from Werowocomoco on the Pamunkey (York) River. In his quest to expand his influence, he relied upon the spiritual advice of Uttamatomakkin, the Powhatan head shaman who had the power to communicate with the influential spirit world. His success was so manifest that to ignore advice from the gods who had guided him here would be irresponsible.

The Powhatan revered many gods, among them Okeus. Whether he had been there always, had been imported, born of the parental gods, or had arisen with social complexity will always be unclear. He played the destroyer to Ahone's creator. He brought on sickness and disaster, punished people for their wrongdoings, and attacked humans as a violent force of nature. He also would bring prophecies, signs of apocalypse that may be seen yet not understood, such as a new star.

Even something as eternal as a god is subject to change. In 1607, Okeus was about to challenge three centuries of Powhatan hegemony. His approach to destroying humankind this time seems to have shifted not long before the English landed. The natural disasters of memory were behind the Powhatan, but regular sails on the horizon were points of light they could not ignore. The disaster coming at them in that year was social, and now Okeus' approach reflected the status of the Powhatan as the preeminent power in the tidewater. The tensions a people face as they grow toward empire can play out in the way their god believes in them.

One night Uttamatomakkin and four or five other shamans, all of whom spoke a sacred language unknown to the uninitiated, were at worship in his temple, which stood in the oak and hickory forest outside Werowocomoco. They had been summoned by one of their gods. To enjoy communion with the god, Uttamatomakkin ritually painted his entire body black and tied to his ear a garter snake, which twined slowly about his face during the ceremony. The ablutions of worship and conjuration called for him to bring forth and explore visions, so he lowered his face into the smoke of aromatic herbs burning in a fire. (The mixture is unknown, but it undoubtedly included tobacco.) A vision came to the shaman. A warrior appeared in the air. He was of mythic proportion. He was beautiful. Half of his head was shaved in the fashion of a warrior, and the lock on the left fell to the ground; his arrow and bow were majestic. Uttamatomakkin knew this god. It was Okeus, and he had come with a warning.

Far away, beneath another god, the night hung from a new star.

There, on London's Blackwall docks, amid the riggings, voices, clatter, and passengers, no one liked the apparition. The new star was ominous. No one in living memory had seen it before; Sir Edmund Halley would name it for himself when it returned close to a century later, marking changes below with continuity in the cosmos. The star warned the superstitious men of impending catastrophe, but there was no way to stop the misadventure now ahead of them and across the ocean.

The men lumbered and loaded their three ships with dogs, barrels of shot, ordnance, muskets, pikes, lances, helmets, chest plates, armor, and enough food—grain, hogs, salted beef and pork—for five full months. The ships' rosters listed a hundred men and four boys. Among other missions, the men were expected to replicate English society, with its structure, in the Virginia woods. Almost half of the men were therefore gentlemen, souls of refinement whose only mission, it would seem, was to be estimable. Those who would estimate them later, and dourly at best, were carpenters and bricklayers and soldiers. Others were bad boys of privilege whose parents were sending them thither to let hard work and adventure make men of them. Laboring among them, booted, bearded, and arrogant, was one man who thought himself the most competent individual onboard, a mad mercenary of a man, who was also one of the founders of this venture, the Virginia Company. He remained inconspicuous, however. The men on dock and deck knew only of the other founders—Bartholomew Gosnold, the colony's driving dreamer, Christopher Newport, and Edward Maria Wingfield.

The Virginia Company was founded in a time of intellectual upheaval. There can be no doubt that the ideas of the high Renaissance influenced and inspired the men to dream beyond their philosophy of life. The popular playwright William Shakespeare was even then masterfully dramatizing the modern human individual—a character with a breadth and depth of internal conflict inside societies, one capable of seeing the invisible architecture of fate and searching for a doorway out. Such thinking was in the atmosphere above the founders of the Virginia Company. Although their mission was ostensibly commercial, its most enduring product would be personal. In January 1607, the *Susan Constant*, the *Discovery*, and the *Godspeed* sailed down the Thames toward Atlantic storms. Few of the men aboard would live much longer, yet the fault was not in the comet.

Six weeks passed as they rocked on violent water in the channel at the edge of the Atlantic, unable to sail farther, and ate deeply into their provisions; the planned five-week crossing proved too optimistic. Something of a crisis loomed onboard. The men wanted to quit. A vote was taken. All agreed but one—a preacher who lay dying of what they undoubtedly believed was seasickness. He alone raised his hand to carry on. The decision was made: if he, the sickest one of all, wanted to continue, then they all would. Unfortunately, six months would show that the preacher did not suffer from motion sickness—and though we will never know what he had, many seemed to contract the man of god's illness and die amid the dry green of an alien forest. He had killed them all with a wave.

As the winter storms abated, the ships began to move. They sailed south until "the butter melted" and then turned right, the common directions given then for sailing to the Canary Islands. From those islands they then launched out across the Ocean Sea, newly christened the Atlantic. At some point during the long crossing, a quarrel broke out between two men; the specifics are lost to history, since no one captured the byplay, Edward Maria Wingfield, a wealthy merchant, won the debate. The mad mercenary, the bearded braggart, was put into leg chains and cast into the brig. With his back to the ship's rolling wall, he lapsed into a state of explosive calm. He lost the argument not because he was wrong—he was always right, in his view—but because he was only a captain. It always came down to rank. Faced with injustice, he could be a vengeful man and he could wait—and none of the gentlemen sleeping above him knew how long he could wait. If there was one serious problem, it was this: the charge was mutiny, and the penalty, death.

In the smoky daylight of his longhouse,

Wahunsunacock and his brother Opechancanough listened to Uttamatomakkin's telling of the prophecy. Scholars believe twin chiefs governed the Powhatan: Wahunsunacock was the paramount chief and peace chief, and Opechancanough, the war chief. While Wahunsunacock oversaw the internal affairs of the Powhatan coalition, some scholars believe Opechancanough ran the offensive strategy against foreign invaders. Though years apart in age, the brothers had risen together in power.

The prophecy was ominous. Okeus had warned that a new tribe would settle on the bay, become powerful, and destroy the Powhatan.

The Powhatan leaders knew of these people. They lived down by the shores of the bay. Traditionally, when the Powhatan made war on another tribe, they would kill the men and bring the women and children back to build their population. This time, however, Wahunsunacock and Opechancanough made a radical decision. They would not spare a single person—man, child, or woman. The prophecy Okeus had revealed was too terrible and required extreme measures. Okeus could not be doubted.

By this time, both brothers had lived three times through the near extinction of their people. The brothers claimed that countless times they had come upon towns and villages peopled with the dead and dying, black vomit staining their bodies and deerskin skirts and leggings. The scene was the medical equivalent of a meteor blast, and only recently, in wide array, had the survivors rebuilt their nation. Some scholars speculate that this meant that illnesses of foreign import—the viral infections of the French, Spanish, English, and Africans—had swept north into Powhatan territory and had decimated its population almost below a point of élan vital. There is no archeological evidence to support this interpretation, however. Ironically, the Powhatan nation was named Tsenacommacoh, meaning "densely inhabited land."

When Opechancanough returned that day to the Pamunkey nation, where his brother had installed him as their chief, or werowance, his mission was to gather the warriors from all the tribes of the Powhatan paramount chiefdom—a total force of about two thousand. They would launch down the river, feign trade with the invaders, and once inside, attack. The skirmishes would end in near annihilation. The Powhatan would prevail.

The English, still quarreling, had no idea what was going on.

And yet not every apocalypse falls from the sky. Some arrive as quietly as a turn in the breeze.

IN THE FOLLOWING MOMENTS, THE E N O R M I T Y

OF NEW SHIPS MAY HAVE COME OVER WAHUNSUNACOCK, AND HE MAY

HAVE WATCHED

THE WORLD OF HIS PEOPLE

IN MOTION AROUND HIM.

2

In the last years of his life,

the leader of the Powhatan people made a decision that would leave
him grasping for control of the nation he had built—and which
would in a few inconceivable decades send his people moving away
into the woods. The decision was not popular then, or later—but
more telling than his decision to let the English live, perhaps, is the
way he hesitated, at first, to make any decision at all. His hesitation
echoes in the lives of a people who were the first to succumb to the
vast Native American diaspora—a compound dispossession of land,
culture, language, and identity resulting in a genocide that began on
their rivers and still continues in myriad ramifications today.

The attack on the tribe in the bay was a success; the newcomers,
however, were not the English; they were the Chesapeake. The
several hundred settlers on the perimeter of Tsenacommacoh, in
and around today's Norfolk and Virginia Beach, did not survive the
Powhatan onslaught. The Powhatan could now relent: the prophecy
had warned them, the chief's actions had been decisive, and the
nation was now safe from disease and invaders.

The English, meanwhile, were exploring the small Caribbean

island, Mona. As Powhatan tomahawks came down, English boots went up mountains, in search of fresh water. As Powhatan knives severed scalps and heads, the English buried a man who died with "his fat melted out of him." As the Powhatan set Chesapeake villages ablaze, the English wandered through villages devoid of life. (The Spanish had carted off the indigenous people en masse, sending them to die as slaves in their Caribbean plantations.) As the Powhatan warriors hung their war trophies, the English raised a cross on the North American coast, sinking to their knees in the sand in gratitude. After five months at sea, their provisions depleted, they had met with men and women who had emerged from the forest bearing baskets of food and fruit, and saw them as living in Eden. The friendliness would not last. One night, native men fired arrows; the English fired musket shot. They returned to their ships and sailed until they found an island twenty miles upriver from the ocean, beyond the view of Spanish warships that occasionally patrolled the coast.

As we continue to add flesh to the bones of our knowledge of

the Powhatan, we can visualize the fateful day when Wahunsunacock received news of the arrival of foreign ships inside his nation. For the Powhatan and other aboriginal people, sweeps of recurring themes and events balanced their societies with the revolving seasons. So that May morning dawned with a sense of continuity as others had for centuries. What the Powhatan would do throughout the next year had been done as well for centuries. They knew war and starvation, disease and violence, but they knew also the shelter of deep continuity. Although we can never know what they thought and felt—and to guess too closely would be presumptuous and misleading—we can conceive that their experience of life within the sphere of water and forest and divinity embraced a depth of being that was ancient in its origins. This view of them is crucial—because what had arrived beyond the central plain and on the far side of the

next southern peninsula were not just three English ships.

Other ships had arrived without much incident, but what lay deep within the English cargo was a foreshortening of time, an imperative to change, a death knell to continuity. It would come toward them like a tsunami, but rather than recede, this inundation would roll over them for centuries.

That mid-May morning, the sunrise was brisk and chill over the Pamunkey (York) River. The river, with its origins in the Blue Ridge, was roiling with spring floods, its surface marbling. Every morning, with a communal ease born of a shared ritual centuries old, hundreds of people of every age came down to the river to bathe. The air was plain; voices carried across the water. The men and women were segregated a short distance apart. Both sexes sprinkled tobacco upon the waters in a spiritual observance before beginning their ablutions; the children splashed and slapped at the water, and explored.

Their skin, as colonist William Strachey later described, was lively with tattoos that encircled their arms, breasts, and bodies with colorful images of flowers and snakes and birds. Upstream, the men were shaving their chins with shells. When called upon, the women plucked the men's hair and used reeds and mussel shells to shave their heads—either half or its entirety, which allowed their hair to fall long only on the left, freeing up their bow hands—and then did the same for the children. In the eyes of colonist Robert Beverley, Powhatan women were "generally beautiful, possessing an uncommon delicacy of shape and features." They smoothed walnut oil into their hair to leave it sleek and shiny "like a raven's wing." They applied oil of bloodroot to their skin, tracing a thrilling flush from the tips of their fingers across their chests; they also applied the oils to the children—the colonials speculated that these oils, as well as the sun, deepened the color of their skin. Some women, having finished bathing, filled their clay pots with water and slowly made their way up the path toward the capital town.

We only need watch the movement of women's hands in these mild routines of morning to see the deep lines of continuity that

braid the community. By following the way the women touched their own bodies, the men and the children, the seeds, plants, hides, flints, feathers, cornmeal, and meat, we can trace the ways in which the women physically connected everyone to everything important and sewed their collective lives into a resilient material. The female sphere of affection, continuity, and celebration—a psychological gathering of the ancestral and the yet-to-be—balanced the male sphere of hunting and fighting.

That spring morning, Wahunsunacock stood up to his knees in the water, bathing among the families, when two men in a canoe drew a current of glossy silence toward him. Everyone took notice, pausing briefly in their routines to watch. One of the men in the canoe was Rawhunt, a man whom the English always credit for his skill and intelligence in negotiations.

The news was brief. The newcomers had settled, rather stupidly, on an island devoid of fresh water, one so foul with swamp and mosquitoes that few people went there. They wore heavy coats like the Spanish, but whereas the Spanish were militaristic

and adept, these men appeared clumsy and argumentative. They had not built a camp yet, but slept under the trees; nor did they fish or hunt. Stranger still, they had no women with them, so they must be poor, for only the poor cannot afford two or three wives. (What kind of man travels without a woman to make life livable?) It was also said that they had skirmished with men from the Nansemond tribe.

In response to this report, Wahunsunacock didn't say anything; a sense of disquiet about the new ships came over him as he watched the world of his people in motion around him—the women naked and unashamed, full of grace, bathing or fetching water; the children playing along the shore and splashing in the shallows; the men standing at a respectful distance. To see Wahunsunacock as vulnerable at that moment, caught unawares in his morning ablutions, would be a mistake. If the English shared any response to this historical man, it was their amazement for his stature and presence. He was not only taller than they by far, but he was well framed and supple with muscle in his torso and legs from a life of running miles in the woods, of eating and fasting, fighting and loving. He was more than equal to the English in strategy and negotiation, politics and war—power and presence manifest in a man.

Wahunsunacock climbed to the top of the bluff overlooking the river. He stood a while in a glade of loblolly pines, looking in the direction of the far side of the peninsula. He could see the southern expanse of his nation streaming through the morning. In the twenty years since the Powhatan tribes had joined efforts to drive out the Spanish, he had grown his six inherited tribes into a powerful coalition of thirty-two tribes. This nation, Tsenacommacoh, had just come together, however; it was still fractious. If new invaders were up one of his rivers, he had a lot to think about, especially if they were not the Spanish.

At this moment of his life, Wahunsunacock stood on the summit of his power. If the English later found him majestic and powerful, then for those who lived under his dominion he was even more imperial. In some smooth array all around him lay the lives of some 15,000 or even 20,000 people in thirty-two tribes, and in many his blood was flowing. Each time he brought a tribe under his control, he removed their leader, placed one of his own in charge, and then married the queen and attempted to produce a child or children by her, thus endowing all the various people beneath him with his genetic influence. The English later guessed his offspring numbered about a hundred. He was not the first leader of his people to practice this kind of statecraft—which is, indeed, found everywhere—but he was the first to take the name of his tribe for his title—Chief Powhatan—and then give it as the collective name of his people.

The new name signaled a depth of combined being with his people. When the English arrived they found not only a mortal with a given name—Wahunsunacock—but one venerated by his people as someone who was half-human and half-divine and who bore their name for his own. Essentially, he *was* the people. Moreover, if divinity bestows immortality, then Chief Powhatan enjoyed this, too, for through so many offspring his reach into the genetic future of his people would become infinite.

As Wahunsunacock grew in stature and power, he assumed more than the history and spirituality of his people; he also gained control over the way decisions were made. In his youth, when the nation had six tribes, he was obligated to seek ideas and advice from all of his chiefs—the werowance (men) and werowansqua (women)—when a decision needed to be made whether to fight or negotiate. But Wahunsunacock had succeeded brilliantly in growing his nation, and a result of this ambition was now on the political plateau all around him that May morning. The Powhatan paramount chiefdom had become so large and far-flung that distance compelled him to consolidate the decision-making power in himself alone and heed only the spiritual guidance of his shamans. He alone was the font of the Powhatan spiritual force whose energy rose through him and flowed into his political appointments, bringing success to them all.

Cultures often come to critical tipping points in their rise, and when faced with radical pressures, they can continue to act the way they always have, or they can consider new ideas and try to master their tribulations—and be reborn in the process. In the past, such as when the Spanish had ventured up the Powhatan River, the old way—meet the enemy with force—worked well. But, if what Wahunsunacock was now hearing was correct, then these new invaders were not the Spanish. Rather than rout these newcomers, as tradition dictated, what the Powhatan could do this time is use them, and try to leverage them against the more assertive enemies on the nation's frontiers. Powhatan could become a player with an international presence, and use these fumbling men to acquire weapons and wealth. He might manipulate them into helping him extend and consolidate the reach of his power to places otherwise unattainable—even, perhaps, beyond the mountains.

In his new mantle of power and decision-making, Powhatan was omnipotent: there was no one to tell him, "No." He could have asked Opechancanough for advice, but he already knew what his brother's response would be. His brother enjoyed a hatred for the Spanish and would want to kill these new invaders right away. But Powhatan had other ideas—he was able to envision more than a nation, he saw an empire. If they did not yet have the permanent buildings of people like the Aztec, he nevertheless had the energy and intelligence to bring a new state of that scale into being. From the bluff where he stood in the rising glare, an empire of that scope may have been only a hundred years away. The possibility was founded on and fostered by the agricultural ingenuity of the women and the expansive trade sustained by their products.

It is unlikely that Powhatan saw his people as poised on a precipice,

good or bad; nevertheless, he was thinking of politics. His nation was strong, yet writhing with discontent. Faced with an invading force, the people could still do things the old way—pack up and fade into the forest. The people under his control paid him tribute, and in times of need and hunger, his power flowed from

his given authority to take these tributes and redistribute them as he saw fit, blending compassion with leverage. The political authority of his people came to the sons and daughters through the mothers' line, so in a sense Powhatan's power of redistribution came from the military vitality of male culture and from the nurturing responsibility of the female culture—though the latter is not customarily seen as a source of political power. These two cultural imperatives—to make war or to feed—would play into the confused policy regarding the best way to get rid of the English.

The Powhatan chiefdom reflected its mosaic distinctions, and the unbearable pressure for change brought on by the English would pit man and tribe against one another to answer the demands of military vitality and agricultural replenishment. The Chickahominy, for instance, paid Powhatan a reluctant yearly tribute to maintain peace between the two tribes, but they would not let Powhatan install an outside chief. They later would ally with the English to Powhatan's disadvantage. Of all the people the English met, the Chickahominy were the most openly contemptuous of Chief Powhatan, and described him as cruel. Others might have agreed.

Such pressure would strain the Powhatan coalition, the largest and most powerful chiefdom along the Atlantic seaboard when the English arrived. The nation that Powhatan had grown since the late 1500s spanned an estuarial world from the Potomac River south to the James River and from the Fall Line east to the Eastern Shore. It opened the four rivers of that withered alien handprint into an encompassing human hand—the Potomac, the Rappahannock, the Pamunkey, and the Powhatan (James), as well as the Eastern Shore. The blast of eons earlier had created the rumpled meteor hills and flats where they lived, the beds of freshwater streams that supplied their towns, the aquifer below that fed the streams, the glass beads that laced the forest and glowed in necklaces, and a terrain that they cleared into meadows for crops. The Powhatan enjoyed the bounty of centuries of created and inherited wealth—attractive resources to neighboring nations and unallied tribes.

On the political map to the north of the Powhatan were the Massawomec and the Patowomec, who lived along the Potomac River, a name that means either "river of swans" or "the place to which tribute is brought." The Powhatan paid tribute to these and other tribes on the river, including the Massawomec and the Nacotchtank, southern paws of the Iroquois nation, which directed the Potomac area tribes in raids of attrition against the Powhatan, and rarely made peace. The Iroquois themselves, as well as the Susquehannock, would sometimes sweep down from the north, their raids yielding ferocious legends of cannibalism and other horrors. To the south, below the Powhatan River, were the Nansemond and the Meherrin, both of whom antagonized the Powhatan with raids. And finally, to the west, near the Blue Ridge, were the Monacan, with whom the Powhatan traded in goods and skirmishes. Tension between the two peoples meant that the Monacan were an unreliable source of copper for the Powhatan. As the Spanish and English wanted gold, the Indians wanted copper, and the Monacan had sacred mines of copper around the circumference of their nation.

Powhatan figured that if the English could give him copper, he would ask them to help him subjugate the Monacan. English copper would give him wealth and status, just as English swords and guns would give him a military advantage in running conflicts. Powhatan could soon introduce his rivals and nemeses to their own foreshortened timeline. He would engage the English by his own rules, and they would return the favor, by their own. And he might have had even larger ambitions.

He may have been contemplating a chance to expand his boundaries beyond the Blue Ridge, into the valley of Shenandoah, meaning "daughter of the stars." If he could position himself as the broker on the Atlantic coast for European goods, he could leverage that exclusivity into enormous power. Indians in the American South and near West already enjoyed European goods and tools, which had been scavenged from a century of shipwrecks along the southern coast and pipelined into trade routes. By focusing beyond the western mountains, he could build an empire.

Normality greeted Wahunsunacock on his return to Werowocomoco, the capital town of the chiefdom. The town's inhabitants were preparing for the day ahead. Still damp from their bath and dressed only in fringed deerskin skirts— some wore full-length mantles decorated with shells, paint, and fringes—the women dealt with their hair. It was coarse, heavy, and black; they roped it in a bun or let it fall down their backs. They conditioned it with animal grease to keep it out of their way while they toiled in the public fields and private gardens.

The men, dressed in moccasins, skirts of leather, and deerskin leggings for ease of travel through tall grass and forest, went about their business. Some wore the wings of a hawk or buzzard across their backs; rattlesnake rattles attached to their ears clattered with their motions and the wind, entertaining them and reminding them of their bravery in having killed the beast for his music. They had great holes in their ears, two or three, and from these dangled chains of pearl or copper, and even garter snakes, which twined about and amused them with exploratory kisses upon the lips. A rare few men wore dead rats from their ears.

Forty of fifty men prepared for the day's deer hunt with another tribe. They painted their skins with an ointment made from *puccoon*—the powdered red root of the orange flower by that name— to shield themselves from lice, ticks, mosquitoes, and the sun. In the hunt ahead, they would set a circle of woods on fire, and then close in slowly around the herd of deer and use their long bows and arrows to bring them down. The hunt was for the celebration that night,

timed to give thanks for the new season. They had a circle of carved masks, and would sing and dance around it as they had for hundreds, possibly thousands, of years.

The children ran naked with impunity and played; the girls, most of all, toyed with shell beads. Powhatan stopped outside his sixty-foot longhouse in the center of town and watched the abundance of children turning cartwheels, which was a favorite activity of theirs. His eye followed the antics of one child in particular. She was a singular girl, curious and spirited—a combination of willful and playful in which he might have recognized his own intellectual propensities. As a child and a girl, she would have fallen far outside the art or practice of power. Yet it is poignant that, of the hundreds of children the English would meet, her name stands out among them.

She was nine or ten when the English arrived, though some thought she might have been twelve or older. During their passage from birth to death, the Powhatan people received several names. One was given at birth, another was given for spiritual reasons, and still another singled out that essence that makes the individual unique. The girl in flight just then, and who may have lived her earliest years with her mother among the Pamunkey or Mattaponi people, had been given the birth name Matoaka and the spiritual name Amonute. It was Powhatan's prerogative as a male—and her father—to give her a nickname. She came in front of him, tumbling hands over heels; he caught her up and swung her over, struggling in his arms. He called her Pocahontas.

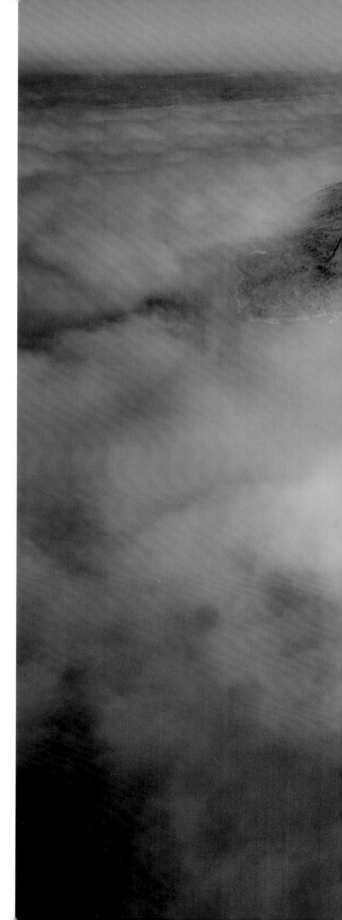

THE ISLAND

WAS FEATHERY AND MILD...

THE FOREST WAS MADE OF TALL, GOOD TREES,
AND ITS CORRIDORS WALKED AWAY FROM THEM INTO

ALLURING CASCADES

OF MAY SUNSHINE.

After five months on
water and a hundred
years in mind, the men from England finally
sank their anchors into the mud of the Powhatan River, which they
named the James. They waded ashore with a few advance reports,
maps, supplies, weapons, and a collection of hopes, dreams, and
agendas. With every step they got lost—not geographically but
culturally, and the ensuing disorientation would continue for
years. One and all they did not believe they had left England far
behind—but English culture would not survive in this landscape.
And though they had arrived in Virginia, a land claimed and named
by earlier English explorers for the virgin Queen Elizabeth, the
destination before them was still unknown and alien.

   The island they explored was feathery and mild. Their shoes
spilled water. They walked about the grassy spaces of light. The forest
was made of tall, good trees; its long corridors walked away into
alluring cascades of sunshine. Sprays of yellow splashed the green.

The scenery they lifted their faces into was more than a cathedral of impressions. Awash in the floral silence and scented stillness of this May morning, and with the memories of topless women bringing them baskets of fruit—the later clash with a few men considered a minor inconvenience—they decided that Paradise was real and they had found it in Virginia. For those among them who had known life on great estates, and those acquainted with Shakespeare, these first views of such freshness inspired a poetic impulse—a romantic sensibility toward the landscape that would remain with the Virginians throughout their troubled history.

The mission, nevertheless, was uppermost in the men's minds. Even while admiring the forest's beauty, President Edward Maria Wingfield made quick assessments of the trees, his mind filling with ideas. Unlike the Spanish who had come to this coast on behalf of their king, these men from England were here on behalf of a company, in search of business opportunities. Wingfield noted that vertical lumber was available and plentiful in the form of hickory, oak, cypress, and other hardwoods. He also eagerly anticipated finding ready gold somewhere in the shadowy interior, a waterway to the Far East, and even a few survivors of the Roanoke colony lost back on the coast some thirty years earlier. These goals were all part of their assigned mission, as well as converting the local pagans to Christianity.

The English already had accomplished, to the best of their knowledge, the mission's first two objectives. First, since the Spanish also laid claim to this land, which they called La Florida, the English had settled upriver beyond the view of Spanish ships scouting the coast. Second, they had lowered the anchors in a spot the Indians did not use, thus avoiding trespassing on Indian lands and irritating them; and fortuitously, only a slim elbow of land connected the island to the mainland, so they easily could defend themselves against any Indians should the occasion arise. With these initial objectives met, they could move on to the immediate business of bringing English law up out of the holds, and the law had to be satisfied.

Wingfield ordered a few men to bring the man in the brig ashore. The man's ill-tempered words back at the Canaries had won him the charge of mutiny, a hanging offense. More comments in the same abrasive key had inspired the building of gallows on the Caribbean island of Nevis a few weeks previously, but the accused, as he later wrote, could not be "persuaded" to use them. Here, though, among the trees, Wingfield spied a few good limbs that could serve the purpose well. The mission's entire company of men—cabin boys, carpenters, farmers, wastrels, gentlemen—gathered to watch, some faces mirroring indifference, others a sporting interest. The largest group of men who had come over, the highborn, stood around the president. Most of these men believed that, as the Spanish had done in the West Indies, they soon would lord over plantations and then triumphantly return to England fat and buoyant on New World success; such a life was due them as a perquisite of their social status. If one among them thought the prisoner falsely accused, no one spoke in his defense. This would be an easy mission, after all, and there was no reason for them to suffer the arrogance and insolence of this odious little man. He was simply and luridly beneath them.

The prisoner smelled like a dead hog. His beard was wild. His clothes were foul. And at only five foot one, he was quite short. He was an obstinate and unrepentant soul, even after thirteen weeks in the brig and facing execution. Indeed, as he stood in front of them in chains, waiting to be hanged, Captain John Smith probably looked like he was ready to murder Wingfield and the sops and fops around him, a few of whom may have shifted uneasily while retaining that caricatured air of condescension. To Captain Christopher Newport and a few others, though, another edge was visible in the condemned—a strange gift for composure at the worst moment. It was an ability honed by a series of life experiences that were equally responsible for his being in the New World.

John Smith was born in 1580

in Lincolnshire, and grew up adventuring throughout the brook, field, and forest of his father's farmlands. His father was successful in farming; he gave young Smith the grammar school education that was common for those families with aspirations for their children. Smith seems to have been precocious and energetic, bright and direct in all he did. His energy and drive caught the attention of a benefactor, Lord Willoughby—the first of several people of high social position who became so charmed by the stocky, handsome boy with witty eyes and an attractive smile that they would help him as much as possible, compelled, perhaps by his liveliness, to intervene on his behalf.

When Smith was fifteen he followed form by going to work as a merchant's apprentice, but the routine was suffocating; upon his parents' deaths, he was free to follow his own desires. At the time, King Philip II of Spain was conducting a holy war against the Low Countries; as many other boys and men were doing, Smith joined the fight. After three years, he left the war during a lull, traveling through France to return home. He set about remaking himself: he camped in the woods, reading old books, educating himself on the new technology of making war with gunpowder, studying languages and strategies—in short, he took himself away from the world to prepare to launch himself into it again.

He succeeded with aplomb. The war between Catholics and Protestants in the Low Countries had sickened him with its hypocrisy, so this time he went to more distinctive battle lines: the European frontier of ranges and forests where Muslims warred with Christians. He proved himself invaluable to any army he joined, conjuring up successful schemes for turning back the Turks. He was awarded his coat of arms and the commission of captain. And then disaster befell him, and his history begins to shine with mythic overlays.

The Turks captured him and threw him into slavery. In Turkey,

he attracted the eye of a noble woman, Charatza Trabigzanda, who, Smith later wrote in his autobiography, saw in him something she enjoyed and decided that she would like to have for herself. She pulled him out of the slave ranks. He may have become her lover. She treated him well, and even had ideas for his future. Many people will tell you that this is the first grand falsehood that Smith invented. These critics claim that his being saved by a powerful woman—and he claimed to have been saved by quite a few—is nothing more than an old literary device and one that he would use again with Pocahontas in the starring role.

They may be right; nonetheless, it is worth noting that it is not unheard of for a wealthy woman wishing to exercise her power in the social realm to rescue an artist or charming man if she finds him desirable, and then remake him by her own design. Stories of the colonization of the New World often hinge on female power. Christopher Columbus and Queen Isabella, Sir Walter Raleigh and Queen Elizabeth, Smith and Pocahantas—the stories grew in some part from a psychological dynamic that combines male adventure, female power, and an implicit sexual energy. To dismiss Smith's myriad stories because they fit an archetype is to risk blinding ourselves to the power of influential women and the way they labor to transform a few good males into successful men, all to ensure the future of the group.

Regardless of whether all his picaresque tales can be confirmed, Smith's personality does precipitate his survival. Some aspect of his character fascinated and intrigued people, far more for women than men. They wanted to be around him, to bask in his strength, or to savor his conversation and confidence. When it served a purpose, Smith sheathed his antagonism in charm. He was clearly a forceful personality with many adventures, not unlike Othello, who did woo Desdemona with the mighty magic of his stories; and once he was fallen and vulnerable, this aggressive but injured little man might have been irresistible.

Charatza decided to free Smith and to transform him into a better man. But Smith was not really free. She sent him to her brother to learn how to run a plantation, but he only received beatings at her brother's hands. One day, Smith had had enough. When the brother raised his whip against him, Smith caught the whip, pulled the brother to the ground, and killed him. He put on the dead man's clothes, swung onto his horse, and escaped the plantation.

He made his way into Russia, went south into Europe, sailed with a French privateer along the coast of North Africa, and then returned to London. He trooped the streets with that seething sense of eagerness and anxiety all too familiar to men who come home from war and find themselves unable to reacclimate to their previous lives. London was a vision of hell. The coal and wood fires of thousands of chimneys cast ashen veils across the day's morning face. The slums filled with farmers who had been thrown off their land, and taverns roistered with whoring rogues who had fought for any army that would have them. Smith was one of these men, but he was different. He was a braggart, but one who read arcane books and was always educating himself; he may have seen the hit of the 1606 season, Shakespeare's *Macbeth*, playing to clamorous crowds in the Globe Theater. (Later, Smith may have felt his paranoid dinners with Chief Powhatan eerily paralleled the play's reduced outline of a revered dinner guest murdered by his host.) Smith was restless; he soon became involved with the founding of the Virginia Company.

The opportunities and adventure the company would afford appealed to Smith, but it would be a mistake to cast a romantic light on his ambition without delving into his darker side. It is dangerous to use hindsight and play psychiatrist, but if one considers that Smith's adventures in Virginia are a compound reaction against his traumas in Europe, then much is revealed. From what we can glean in his autobiography and writings by his contemporaries, his behavior from London onward seems to present the classic symptoms of post-traumatic stress disorder, a modern diagnosis with ancient descriptions. The diagnosis of PTSD was first given to twentieth-century soldiers, men who repeatedly witnessed unspeakable carnage, saw their comrades dying all around them, and were nearly killed. But the disorder is not limited to soldiers: anyone can suffer PTSD after being raped, mugged, held hostage, tortured, threatened with execution, or after experiencing other harrowing events.

A long list of adverse effects afflict people who suffer from this kind of severe psychological injury. Survivors may not feel emotions as others do, especially those of intimacy, tenderness, and sexuality. They may have a foreshortened sense of their future, with no hope for a career, marriage, or children. They may feel estranged from other people and have a heightened vigilance, an increased startle response, and sudden outbursts of rage. If they crave excitement, it is because it makes them feel alive, or feel calm and in control. Their thoughts may be chaotic; brimming with manic energy, they are often incapable of lying except to save their lives.

Smith may have exhibited all these signs and more of PTSD. His career was chaotic; he was guarded and untrusting; he never married; and he died childless (some scholars even speculate that he was castrated while held by the Turks). He seems to have craved an excitement that would carry him far away from the horrors of war—and the farthest place for him was the New World. For all of his barroom braggadocio, Smith was also vulnerable; the books he would write twenty years after his return from Virginia reveal a range of wounds and losses that make him human and poignant. His wrenching accounts, although exhibiting an often disorganized thought process—another symptom of PTSD—make him far more real and accessible to us than, for instance, Shakespeare. Some scholars say they compose the first self-revealing autobiography, and give him a lasting fame.

This notoriety is due to the fact that we have to see Smith as two men, first as a historical man and second, as a storyteller who created an actor on the page with his name. Their stories are different, ultimately pointing us in two directions. Smith's story is layered with so many mythic blueprints that it is difficult to know

what part was fact and what part myth. Scholars have been able to retrace the historical man's steps, succeeding in verifying names, places, and events—a clear indication that fact underlies much of Smith's autobiography. Other facts present more of a problem. Here is where we meet Smith as a trickster.

This clever fellow, an unpredictable player who knits chaos and order, can talk his way out of trouble and outwit a superior opponent. The trickster dupes you into doing something beyond character, playing on your secret weaknesses. Charming and amusing though he may be, you can never trust his actions or words—which you only realize too late. The trickster appears in many cultures: he is Loki to the Norse, Hermes to the Greeks, Coyote to the Native Americans, Bugs Bunny to millions of children. How cultures esteem the trickster is fundamentally important. In the case of Br'er Rabbit, the story is amiable in Africa, where the sly rabbit eloquently convinces the farmer to let him go, but in Europe, the farmer cares not a whit for his reasoning and kills the palavering hero. The trickster descends most nobly into

human form when Homer renders him as the wily Odysseus, a leader whose relentless grace under fire gets him home again while his panicky crew lays strewn across the years behind him. Smith moved in literary circles on his return to England; it is possible that certain of his adventures began to suggest to him the marvelous outlines of mythology depicted in literature, and the psychological power they have to resonate over time.

Seen through this lens, Smith's tale of his time in Virginia presents crucial scenes in which he plays the trickster, exploring with a band of panicky men a mysterious forest of near giants. The

Powhatan Indians are not mere savages in his stories, but rather enormously powerful adversaries who would kill him and his crew, if not for his sangfroid. All of this was likely true to life, but it is the presentation that matters here—the architecture is the message, and archetype the meaning.

Other colonial writers—William Strachey, Henry Spelman, and George Percy, to name a few—might be more reliable on certain details of Jamestown, because they were cool where Smith was hot; however, they do not stand with the same presence on history's stage. It is only Smith, who writes of cheating death at the hands of his magnificent imperial nemesis, Chief Powhatan, who captures first the imagination of the English and then of the Americans. Admirers and detractors both admit to the power of his storytelling—which may have smoothed history into myth, or found the springs of myth in his personal history. He still captures our imagination because, like Shakespeare, he found that place where myth and history, landscape and memory, combine into a brave new world for every generation.

Smith returned to the scene of his mortality again and again in life and in prose. Having been threatened with losing his life in war and in slavery, he seems to relive that moment over and over in Virginia. Captain John Smith would never make friends, but he would influence his enemies, and his own unique way of dealing with people would rouse in both the English and the Indians a passion to kill him. And though he should have died four or five times, possibly including a plot by the other colonists to murder him, everyone involved would spare his life. In the history of Jamestown, Smith may not be the most pivotal man—a role that falls, eventually, to the mellow John Rolfe—and he may not have saved the colony as often as he claims in his journals, but he probably pushed the colony into jeopardy so often that with an ironic twist, the colonists were compelled to take their own actions to survive both him and their existence in Virginia.

John Smith was a man driven by his convictions, ones that threatened to overturn the English society the colonists tenuously held to in this challenging land. If others in the colony accepted the tacit agreements of the home culture, he did not; he believed in rewarding achievement, not blood. Though grievously born in a disastrous time, his insistence on individual merit over social inheritance would survive and become cultural. He was the first man of American history to stand up to those in command, now rendered as a Man of Action who back-talks the incompetent brass—an archetype and dynamic so omnipresent in works of print and celluloid that such rebelliousness is presented now as a civil right. As with other charismatic leaders, he earned the respect of his men while incurring the wrath of the ne'er-do-wells. They saw a barking little man, and they hated him.

On that May afternoon when Smith stood ready to die,

the Governor called for the box of instructions from the Virginia Company, and its contents were read aloud. To everyone's amazement, the bosses in London had named Smith as one of the colony's leaders, so Wingfield had to pardon him—Smith's first escape as a New World trickster, and second escape from hanging. He had talked back to his superior and gotten away with the insolence. But Wingfield was not happy; he ordered Smith to be chained in the brig for five more weeks.

When Smith stood on the island again, the Edenic scene that he had had little time to appreciate was nowhere to be found. The sky was white. It was mid-June and a torrential haze cast a blaze of heat over everything. Everyone's skin was damp; even wearing cotton jerseys, their heavy pants made them sweat. With temperatures in the nineties, and humidity levels just as high, the Englishmen had never felt anything like the weather in Virginia. A palisade ringed a collection of haphazardly constructed lean-tos, which the men had built after tiring of sleeping under the trees; there was also a lean-to for worship.

Initially, the leaders of the mission had decided against building a fort, believing both that it would look aggressive to the Indians and that their presence was little noticed. In reality, with three ships and colorful clothing, the English were brilliantly conspicuous—as much as Indians arriving in Gravesend, England, would be. After a concerted attack shortly after they arrived and a month of random arrows and a few deaths, they conceded to the reality of local politics—and to the reality of their invasion, which they had disguised to themselves until then as an ostensibly friendly mission. They named the fort, as they had the river, after King James.

The heat exhausted the men, many of whom were also sick; many of them spent their days sitting down in the shade. Smith had been sick but had recovered, and he couldn't help but notice that the laziest of the men were those from good families, as if he and the rest were there to work for them, to build the fort and provide food. This exhibition of supposed superiority angered Smith, fueling his sense of equal opportunity and obligation for all. Of all the things the English originally set sail with—hogs, copper, gunpowder, glass beads, rules, laws, workers, gentlemen, and even rats—the one thing they didn't realize they had imported was this man's cantankerous ideas about a meritocracy, which would soon ignite in a slow-motion explosion the blast radius of which would cover the next few centuries. By midsummer, the condescending fops would begin experiencing their own little paradigm shift. Unknown to them, they were perishing—literally and metaphorically. Smith would be among the few to survive; he

would keep the meritocracy going while their deaths eased away the old social claims to blood privilege.

The men did not understand this land; they were at a loss as to how to survive. Mosquitoes stung; flies bit. The sun gave a pink slap to face and neck; they burned. The swamp breathed with life through frogs and crickets. They fished; that wasn't enough. They needed more food, but their matchlock muskets could not molest the broad side of a ship, much less kill a deer. And they could not figure out why the Indians attacked one day but came to trade the next, unable to see the distinctions between the local inhabitants.

Eventually, a few friendly Indians taught them the political map, and they heard at last of a major nation and of its leader who was known as Chief Powhatan—if they wanted food and peace, they would ultimately have to deal with him. In the meantime, the Indians told them, you might want to cut down the grass around the fort—that's how other Indians are sneaking up on you. So the English finally waded into the high grass, scything it with swords— or a few of them did. The others slumped behind the palisades, where the dying had begun.

Kidney failure began to affect the men. Anemia dulled their eyes and minds and made their arms and legs heavy; the effort of standing made them feel a hundred years old. Their recall collapsed to thirty minutes. And worse was around them: the sickly preacher, whose vote onboard ship was responsible for their continuing to Virginia, may have infected his fellow travelers with his persistent illness. Even if these imported diseases didn't kill them, the local environment was equally detrimental. Just as the American Natives died from European microbes, so did the English from native microbes. (The first three months of a colonial's stay soon became known as "the seasoning"—a time during which the newcomer either acclimated or fell victim to the foreign surroundings. Many did not survive.)

August came on damp and hot; everyone was lying down now, even the workers. This scene was no painterly panorama of men languishing: flies were thick as sunlight; the men's mouths twisted in death, their lassitude salted with water from a possibly brackish well. Summer gave way to autumn winds and a hurricane pressure of something coming at them. Smith was on an edge resembling panic; he saw disaster in the colony's future. Close to half the men were barely alive. Captain Newport, who had set sail for England with a small contingent of men in late June-early July, promising to return by fall, was not back. Someone, literally, had to do something. Smith took charge and led the first notorious raid of his career in Virginia—but not against the Indians.

President Wingfield must have been aghast that night as the men clamored into his quarters and began to ransack his possessions. Smith and others had noticed that, while everyone else was thinning down, the impossible little governor was growing fat. They searched and found, worse than they had expected, a sizeable cache of food and drink. While the men were down to eating gruel with mealy worms, the governor was enjoying the only edible victuals left. They seized and redistributed the food, which did not last long. That night, a vote was taken and Captain John Ratcliffe (aka Ratliff, who had allegedly changed his name from Sicklemore), replaced Wingfield as the governor. In this usurpation of power that night, Smith won the men over entirely—and in a way he would later discover imitated the Indian manner of governance and power.

Smith and Wingfield could not have been more antipathetic. Wingfield had failed twice to see Smith hanged, and Smith had finally sued Wingfield that summer for libel over charges that his constant challenge to authority amounted to sedition. Smith won. Their fighting aside, however, the colony was now in a slough of lethal conditions—a shortage of food and leadership, the chaos of those who seemed to know they were about to die. They had eaten their stores at sea, and when they had opened the last barrels of grain, they found them boiling with worms. Smith's rage went all the way back to London.

With the sublime hubris of those in command far away, the

bosses of the Virginia Company had sent them over with copper and glass beads to trade with, and told them that, if they ran out of food, they should merely ask the locals—whose land they were stealing—to feed them. Smith decided it was time to deal.

He selected nine men and announced that they were heading up the James River to trade with the Indians for corn. It was deep fall in Virginia. Flocks of migrating birds darkened the sky. The tidewater foliage was lush with color and thick with deer. Days away from the fort, far up the Chickahominy River, a tributary of the James, a large hunting party of Indian men left their various villages to conduct a massive hunt and then celebrate. Smith could not have known that, as they sailed up the river with two local guides, they were entering the hunting grounds.

THE RIVER WOUND TIGHTER AND

TIGHTER, THE SIDES CLOSING IN, AND THE FALL OF LOGS AND

LIMBS BEGAN TO BLOCK THE WAY FURTHER

INTO THE UNKNOWN.

Miles away from the slow catastrophe unfolding for the Englishmen on the

swampy island, members of the Powhatan Nation passed summer
and fall in a cyclical routine they had known for centuries, their
lives synchronized to nature's rhythms. However, the presence
of the English weighed on them. Opposing ideas about handling
the invaders began to torque tension between Chief Powhatan
and Opechancanough. As the peace chief and the war chief,
respectively, they considered what they should do. The duality of
the two chiefs was a political mechanism that the brothers used to
steer their nation. The energy of their disagreements would create
a compass they would follow to the end of their lives. In a crucial
sense the Jamestown story must be recast as a tale of these two
men. In their various compensations for one another, they shaped
history and let the English hang on long after political expediency
dictated they should die.

In their meetings, closed to women and children, the men
quarreled. Chief Powhatan saw the English as a possible new

weapon in his arsenal, one that he could use to further consolidate power in his region, and perhaps even extend this reach. Opechancanough did not. In his argument for dispatching the English, Opechancanough returned time and again to the odious example of the Spanish.

The Spanish were a plague. For more than a century, the Castilian stamp of God and gold, silver and slavery was so impressed upon the vast expanse of La Florida that the Powhatan people had heard the horror stories on trade routes. The Spanish colonization tactic was to conquer by fear: simply put, if the natives paid them tribute and converted, they would spare them their swords, torture, and even their hell, which they expounded on in fiery proclamations. Their method aimed to crush the will and aspirations of the individual.

Opechancanough reminded his older brother of a singular person, one who was well known to the Powhatan people. The story of Spanish monstrosity, for them, tapered into a young man named Don Luis.

The English heard the story told often, each time with slight

variations. Essentially, around 1560, perhaps while exploring the woods along the Chesapeake Bay, the Spanish kidnapped a young Kiskiack boy and renamed him Don Luis. Perhaps they grabbed the boy to reinforce fear among the natives, or maybe they wanted an interpreter, one they could indoctrinate and who would help them succeed with the locals and impart the good news of subjugation and salvation.

The story continues that for the next ten years Don Luis lived in a world he never knew existed beyond his woodland empire. Taken to Spain, he saw the majesty and magnificence of Seville, the glory of God writ in stone and circumstance. Philip II patronized him with a royal audience in Madrid. A nice and compliant boy,

he was adept with languages; he studied the Bible. In Mexico City, the colonial name used for the Aztec capital, he saw the breadth of Spanish civilization, and converted to Christianity with his Dominican friars. He spoke of a desire to convert the pagans he had grown up with, to lead them out of the darkness so they would know the joys of salvation. On his first attempt to guide a ship of friars to his homeland, he somewhat inexplicably missed the bay— he had better luck on his second essay.

In 1570, Don Luis settled with the Jesuits in Ajacan, an outpost along the James River, the northernmost line of La Florida. At the time, La Florida rambled south along the Atlantic coastline from the Chesapeake Bay into the West Indies and dissolved in the west somewhere in the grasslands beyond the Mississippi River. We can imagine that in his decade of captivity among the Spanish, Don Luis gleaned a great deal about life in La Florida—and how something on the order of a plague had spread through the region. He heard of how the Taino of the islands had died out in the millions; of how the Aztec had died out in the millions; of how even the great Mississippian people, whose earthen pyramids had seen Spanish soldiers ride their staircases on horseback, were now gone, their cities vanishing into forest overgrowth. Even if Don Luis did not comprehend—or, for that matter, was even aware of—the scope of these occurrences, in his travels from Cuba to Spain to Mexico, and around again, he still had a front row seat to one of history's ongoing and uncompromising genocides—a rarity that eventually lasted in acute slaughter for some three hundred years and encompassed two continents, the land between them, and their sea of islands. Which may explain what happened next.

After a few friendly encounters with the locals, and some very helpful efforts around the outpost at Ajacan, Don Luis began to act strangely, at least to the Jesuits' eyes. He didn't come back as often as he said he would—in fact, the last time he went out to talk

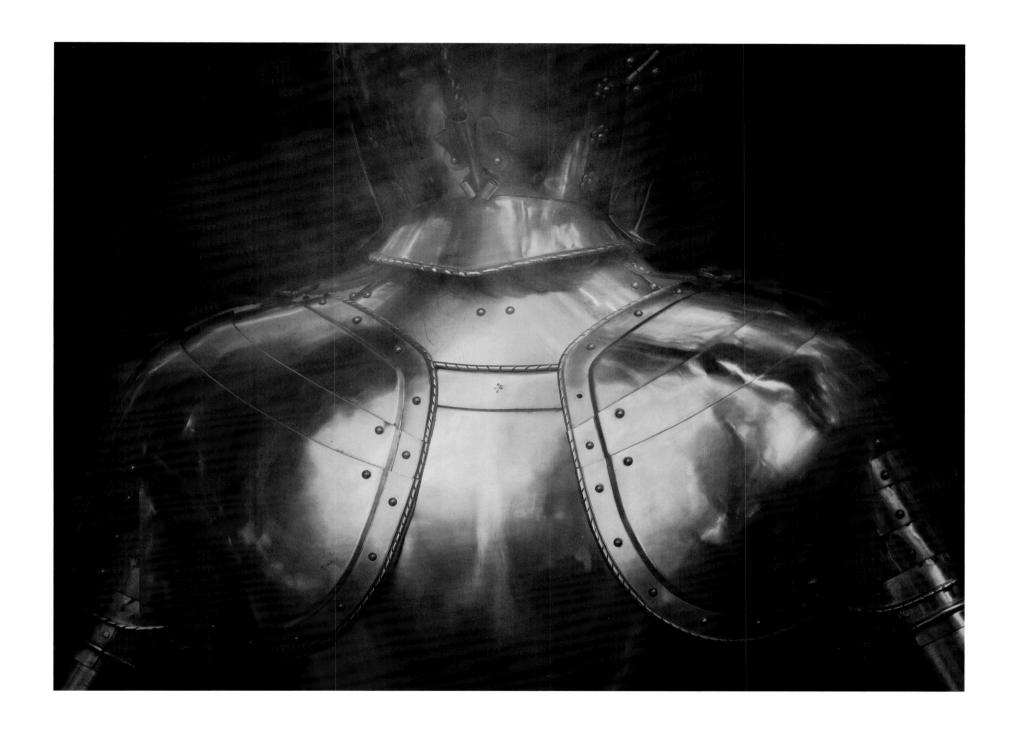

with the locals, he did not return at all. When the friars finally caught up with him several months later, he was back among his tribe and had taken a position of leadership. The Jesuits, by then understandably exasperated with Don Luis, reprimanded him in front of his people. They told him that by taking several wives and assuming power, he was making a joke of his conversion to Christianity, and making their task that much more difficult. Don Luis listened thoughtfully. He returned to Ajacan a few days later—leading a war party.

The Jesuits did not survive. When the Spanish discovered the settlement abandoned and the friars missing, they were enraged. They returned a year later with revenge in mind. This tack was new for them, really, since their previous atrocities had been uncalled for. With smiles and waves from the deck, they lured some of the locals on board to trade, took them hostage, and demanded news of the Jesuits and Don Luis. The locals claimed ignorance of the missing men, further enraging the Spanish, who knew them for liars since they had about them the cloaks and frocks of the men of God. The possibility that these items had been received in trade and that these people were from another tribe apparently did not occur to anyone.

After a while, the Indians admitted that they had heard of Don Luis and of a young Spanish boy named Alonso, presumably spared by Don Luis. The indignant Spanish demanded that Don Luis be returned in exchange for the captives. They also wanted Alonso. Alonso was returned, but not Don Luis. In retaliation, the Spanish hung the Indian hostages from the ship's rigging, in full view of their relatives on shore, and then they turned and fired their cannons on the grieving families. Furious and frustrated with the locals, the Spanish decided that this wasteland without gold was not worth further effort, and sailed. Don Luis had disappeared into the forest and was not heard from again—except in a story handed down as a warning against trusting outsiders.

Chief Powhatan knew well the story of Don Luis.

Just as he had changed his name from Wahunsunacock to Powhatan, and Matoaka had become Pocahontas, Opechancanough had also changed his name. In his youth he had been known as Don Luis.

Again, we find ourselves at a turn where myth and history overlap in the forest between the English and the Powhatan. Scholars note a couple different accounts of Opechancanough's origins: one, that he had come from the southeast; and two, that his father had been from the West Indies, had lived in Mexico, and then had come north into Powhatan country, as the Chickahominy claimed. As a result, historians researching the story of Don Luis theorize several possibilities. First, Opechancanough is the son of Native American Don Luis, sired not long after Don Luis had escaped the Spanish. Second, Opechancanough's father was the Spanish boy, Alonso. Third, Don Luis was altogether unrelated to Opechancanough and Chief Powhatan, but was someone older whom they both knew. Fourth, Opechancanough was Don Luis.

Still another layer of confusion is linguistic, and comes from the vocabulary used to translate certain relationships. For instance, Powhatan and Opechancanough actually may have been first cousins rather than brothers, since the same word was used for both relationships—just as daughter was used to denote niece, as well, meaning that Pocahontas may have been Powhatan's favorite niece, not his daughter.

For romantics, it is tempting, indeed, to cast Opechancanough as the reincarnation of Don Luis, and to use this salient history to motivate some of his bloodlust for the English. The appeal goes beyond motivation, however, to the shape of a story. The point is not the authenticity of detail that lies outside the historic record, but a collective desire to make a communicative pattern—a line of words, a confluence of themes, aural or visual, right or wrong—that will hold the rest in one piece. Research has shown that memory is scored by emotion, so without the surprise twist the story would not impress itself. But when it works, it works—the story passes from person to person, generation to generation. Such a myth codifies a complex truth for those who decode the tale of Don Luis on its myriad levels—historical, metaphorical, spiritual, allegorical, and analogical.

Chief Powhatan recognized the underlying moral of the story of Don Luis; however, he was not convinced that waging war on the foreigners was the right course of action. These new men were not as arrogant, military, righteous, or accomplished as the Spanish raiders who had come before them. And so, Chief Powhatan and Opechancanough came to an understanding. A hundred men who could not feed themselves were not a threat to their force of nearly two thousand men from thirty-two tribes. They would let the English live—but only if they stayed on the island. They would wait and see what the English had in mind. They could kill them later, if need be.

Now, in the waning days of fall, Opechancanough rose up for the hunt. The Powhatan spirit flowed into an abundance of deer; they would find success in the forest. His coterie of fourty-odd men set out southeast into the woods lining the Chickahominy River, a tributary of the Powhatan River. They would rally other men from other tribes, gathering hundreds for the hunt.

About the time the Indian men were hunting en masse, Smith and a crew

of nine were taking the barge up the winding turns of the Powhatan with the aim of bartering for corn with friendly tribes, who became nicer with distance. Smith and his men followed the directions of two guides, who assured them this was the way to Werowocomoco,

home to the chief and the capital town of the Powhatan Nation, yet took them by an indirect way.

The captain and his crew crept deeper into the labyrinthine marshes that were home to the Chickahominy people. The river wound tighter and tighter, the sides closing in. The fall of logs and limbs began to block the way further into the unknown. Smith decided to take two local guides, and Thomas Emry and Jehu Robinson, and head upstream by canoe. He left his men with a final order—stay in the ship.

No sooner had Smith left than the autumn leaves rustled and a bevy of girls—smooth, round, and naked—emerged from the trees. They were singing, "Love you not me? Love you not me?" They were coy and girlish—and smiling. The Chickahominy women that day were the sirens of their time—and their allure says something about the appeal of sudden, unexpected sex that crosses cultural boundaries. Here was the dark edge of colonizing, then and for centuries to come—a chance to find the sensual Eden, where sexuality was not sinful, and the repressions of the Church did not exist—where women were women. Englishmen may have enjoyed the brothel with a sting of guilt, but not anymore. What happened in the New World would stay in the New World—and native women would soon lie supine in every tropic of the British Empire. Behind the rhetorical dress of their declarations, flesh and freedom and trespass called to men. And here is a difference in colonizing: the Spanish would intermarry, blending races; the English would not.

All seven men vaulted overboard, sloshed ashore, and ran after them, and just as adroitly the women spun giggling and vanished into the forest. The men chased them no more than a few yards before a band of local men hidden in the woods leapt on them. The crewmen fought, got loose, and ran to the barge with the Indians in pursuit. All but one reached safety.

George Cassen struggled with his captors, but he was subdued and tied naked to a tree. A fire was built next to him. The locals were preparing to honor him: they would give him a chance to demonstrate his manhood before they killed him. Fundamentally,

both cultures understood the moral value of life; they disagreed on when and why to end it, and on how to frame a noble death. Later, the English would be amazed to see many a Powhatan man executed without making any plea for mercy; however, in Powhatan culture to beg was unmanly, and to scream was worse—a warrior should endure his agony in stoical silence. As the Indians later told them, Cassen got what other men got, no worse than any other Indian caught trespassing. Onboard the barge, his mates listened to every articulate scream.

Using mussel shells, they knifed his fingers off in segments. They began with the smallest joint, moved up by one knuckle on all ten fingers, and tossed the bits into the fire. After his hands were cut down to pads, the men took reeds and, using a quick jerking motion, peeled the skin off of Cassen's face, leaving behind a red mask of fat and muscle and ligature that still worked well enough for him to scream. Next, the men used a flint knife to open his belly. They took handfuls of his intestines, unwound them from the wound, cut them into pieces, and then threw the heaps of offal, fat, blood, and gore into the fire. At some point during his evisceration, Cassen no doubt passed out, or passed into an altered state of consciousness, the dopamine-fueled supreme high of those who experience extreme pain—the likes of which can be seen in footage of lion kills, when the gazelle's eye traces the sky as red muzzles chew inside its body.

This was a moment of spirituality, however, not bestiality, for the Indians. An ancient connective tissue ran through the punishment. In honoring George Cassen that day, the local men performed on him an act of sacrifice with a forgotten yet ubiquitous symbolism. The English warrior gave up his hands, his mask, and his intestinal fortitude to the earth fires, which sent his spirit back into the cosmos. The men onboard the barge did not see it that way. In their eyes, the Indians had proven themselves savages in the unprovoked attack. They could not have imagined that they soon had worse coming to them—from a new English governor, who would kill them for less reason and without honor.

Smith knew nothing of what was going on ten miles back down the river.

His senses were on a serrated edge, no doubt his adrenaline running high—yet this was reassuring to him. He was back in a familiar element of action, danger, and intrigue. He was reliving his military days, to be sure, when he would reconnoiter the enemy's position, each moment charged with the possibility of discovery. In fact, like a spy, he even had a cover story. Although his ostensible mission was to trade for corn, the purpose of his indirect route was reconnaissance. To explain his extreme penetration of their body politic, he would say that he was merely out bird hunting.

Night soon swept down over the Virginia forest, throwing black trees against a violet sky. The four men set camp and built a fire. Smith and the guide went out to scout the area, telling the two men to fire the muskets in alarm if they met with trouble. After searching some time for game, with no luck, Smith and the guide wandered into a swamp. Suddenly, war shouts filled the air, but no muskets were fired.

Smith, realizing he had been led into a trap, grabbed the guide. An arrow struck Smith in the thigh. Two or three men appeared and fired. Smith fired. The musket threw a ball that would bore a hole through a man at twenty yards. In the tight quarters one Indian fell dead, then another. They fired but their arrows fell short; he got off three shots—in about a minute. The woods came alive as two hundred men surged out of the trees, bows drawn. Thrashing in the water, Smith struggled with his guide. He got the man around the neck, wrapped him around the arm with a strap, and used him as a human shield. Under the trees and in the cold water, the standoff began. Fear of his loud weapon gave him a moment of extraordinary advantage.

Smith's guide yelled that this man was a chief. A warrior could be killed, but not a chief. The Indians did not move. Negotiations had begun.

Smith didn't understand what was going on. Through his guide, the warriors told Smith to put down his gun. Smith refused. He began walking, making normal out of the abnormal, as people will, when he lost his footing and fell backward into the mire.

He couldn't reload or get out. Reluctantly, he tossed the useless musket to the ground. Sitting up to his waist in water, he was "nearly dead with cold." Several Indians got him by the arms and hauled him out. They took Smith back to his camp, where they chafed his arms and legs at the fire to keep him alive. Through the flickering light of hunting fires he saw the corpse of Robinson, pierced with some thirty arrows. Emry and the other guide were missing.

An enormous man in leggings and moccasins came toward him. Smith had never seen a man of such a big frame or one as muscular—standing at something over six feet to Smith's five, and lacquered in paint, he was a powerful man among frightening men. At his waist, along with his stone knife and wooden club, rode a tomahawk. The guide introduced him as Opechancanough, the werowance, or chief, of the Pamunkey, and brother of the paramount chief, Powhatan.

We can only imagine what Opechancanough made of the foreigner. Before him was a little bear of a man, who smelled as bad as one. The man had long hair on his face and matted hair down his shoulders, and was disfigured in lumpy clothes; he wore a sleeveless steel shirt that had protected his torso from the arrows. The man had an arrow in his leg, yet did not flinch. (Unknown to Opechancanough, the arrow was caught in the cloth and had only grazed Smith.) The man's stillness was like their stoicism. What did he want?

Smith answered that he was only out…bird hunting.

The guide translated.

Moment followed upon moment. The men prepared a large fire next to a tree, as they had for George Cassen. They tied Smith to a tree; he extended his hand. Opechancanough looked down.

Smith held an object in his palm. Opechancanough poked it with his index finger. Smith watched Opechancanough. The big man poked again at the compass in Smith's hand. The dial was odd to him, moving about as it was, but the glass between the dial and his finger most astonished the big man. The clear barrier was strange and compelling. Smith read the curiosity—How did it work? Why couldn't he touch the dial? Why did it turn? What was it pointing at?—and the wonder in Opechancanough's eyes.

The trickster in Smith seized the moment; he began to speak to his translator, rattling on about North, East, South, and West, nations, races, kings, stars, the moon, and planets. Perhaps more important than what he said was what he did *not* do: beg for his life. Smith was all confidence, and running, maybe, on the high calm that people with traumatic conditioning can feel in a crisis.

Opechancanough hesitated. His brother's will ran toward containment. If Smith were the English chief, then it would be a mistake to kill him. He might have information, be able to negotiate and trade. As for all the palaver, Powhatan ought to hear it himself. Opechancanough measured the little bear and found him lone and wanting, yet not weak and miserable like the others they had killed. He spoke up.

What followed next was a remarkable journey, for the Indians took Smith on an apparently meandering and pointless loop to many of the principal villages of the Powhatan nation. Smith was unaware that his travels were winding symbolically around the nation's edges and moving slowly in toward the center of the Indians' lives, their nation, and, finally, into the longhouse of their leader, where his journey would end in a few more weeks.

We know much of the journey from Smith's own autobiographies, which he would publish some seventeen years later, when back in England. In an ostensibly objective style, Smith wrote of himself in the third person, inserting a cognitive dissonance between the man writing the account and the man who lived it, as though it were still too close to him.

Two days into his captivity, one man tried to kill Smith: the father of a young man whom Smith had killed in the swamp. But the guards protected Smith. That was twice now that the Indians had spared him. Smith was counting. He couldn't figure out why they waited to kill him—or fed him so well, unless it was to fatten him up for a cannibalistic feast. The locals living around the island had said the Iroquois ate their enemies, but Smith had no reason to fear the Powhatan would eat him. But kill him they might.

Word of the captured man spread throughout Tsenacommacoh—the Powhatan chiefdom—to every town and village, perhaps inciting a keen anticipation, a sense of impending change. Upon his arrival at a village, men, women, and children crowded around to see the bear-like man with the wild beard. Smith writes quite vividly of the scene:

"...all the women and children staring to behold him...and then cast themselves in a ring, dauncing...and singing and yelling out such hellish notes and screeches; being strangely painted, everyone one his quiver of Arrowes, and at his backe a club; on his arme a Fox or an Otters skinne...their heads and shoulders painted red, with Oyle and Pocones mingles together, which Scarlet-like colour made an exceeding handsome shew; his bow in his hand, and the skinne or a Bird with her wings abroad dryede, tyed on his head, a peece of copper, a white shell, a long feather, with a small rattle growing at the tales of their snakes tyed to it, or some such like toy...."

Smith's presence was literally extraordinary to the Indians of the Powhatan Nation. For decades they had seen the sails on the water, and had met with the occasional French, English, or Spanish trader, but to have captured an alien chief was an event of surpassing wonder. Smith created a sensation in Powhatan society, and he also impressed his hosts with his potential barbarity and strange implements.

The wonder first directed at the compass soon broadened to include the musket. This object had in one noisy moment killed several warriors. The Indians wondered about the stranger's gods, and whether his gods had shown more favor than their own by giving such a weapon. The truth, as Smith knew, was that muskets were worthless beyond a distance of ten yards, and so when one tribe put him to a demonstration, he surreptitiously broke the French lock rather than reveal how

inferior his weapon was to a bow and arrow. (The myth persists that the English had superior technology in weapons. They didn't. A warrior might fire six arrows in a minute and hit a bird in flight at forty yards. Foreign guns were just atrociously loud. The psychological effects of bizarre, even lethal noise cannot be underestimated, as interrogated terrorists know. We can imagine how formidable and frightening those detonations were to people primarily surrounded by the sounds of humans and nature.)

At each village, Smith was fed and feted; various werowances dined with him and seemed, one and all, to enjoy his company, conversing with him through his guide, who acted as interpreter. One chief told him that people dressed like him lived south of the mountains. (Smith concluded these people could possibly be survivors of the lost Roanoke colony; later, in spite of the chief's directions, they were never found.) Still another chief warned him that although Chief Powhatan would seem friendly, he would cut his throat. That piece of information gave Smith someone to trust, and someone to fear—a position and direction, a social compass, he would never lose. That confidence from one of Powhatan's own chiefs is also the first glimpse we get of Smith's ability to charm people into his sway, of a certain charisma as intense as his later ferocity.

Smith liked to talk, and he talked to anyone who would listen, telling wild and amazing facts, regardless of whether or not they could understand. Once again, armchair caveats apply, but an interpretation of his actions reasons that his insistence on talking to make the abnormal normal, to serenade his captors and forestall his execution, falls in line with the reassuring behavior of those who suffer from Stockholm Syndrome. The kidnapped may be driven by a fear that, if they stop talking, something might then happen. The kidnapped Smith was eager to ingratiate himself to his captors.

One morning, religious men came and performed a ceremony around Smith to divine whether he meant them well or ill; it went on all day, and though he was not killed, he found himself fighting an overwhelming enemy in his nightmares: "Hydeous dreames did

oft see woundrous shapes, Of bodies strange, and huge in growth, and of stupendous makes."

The next day Smith was taken at last, several weeks after being ambushed in the swamp, to Chief Powhatan. In Smith's telling of the story, the meeting unfolded with drama.

> At last they brought him to Werowocomoco, where was Powhatan, their Emperor. Here more than two hundred of those grim Courtiers stood wondering at him, as he had beene a monster…Before a fire upon a seat like a bedsted, he sat covered with a great robe, made of raccoon skinnes, and all the tayles hanging by. On either hand did sit a young wench of 16 or 18 yeares, and along on each side of the house, two rowes of men, and behind them as many women, with all their heads and shoulderes painted red; many of their heads bedecked with the white down of Birds…and a great chayne of white beads about their necks. At his entrance before the King, all the people gave a great shout. The Queene of Appamatuck was appointed to bring him water to wash his hands, and another brought him a bunch of feathers, in stead of a Towell to dry them: having feasted him after their best barbarous manner they could, a long consultation was held, but the conclusion was, two great stones were brought before Powhatan: then as many as could layd hands on him, dragged him to them, and thereon laid his head….

Someone spoke up; it was Pocahontas, who stood among the young women next to the paramount chief. The breach of etiquette was extraordinary, especially for a young girl; later the English would see a warrior get his brains beaten out for simply interrupting a chief while he was speaking. But the English never saw the Indians spank or discipline a child for disruptive behavior—they showed extreme tolerance. Even so, for Pocahontas to call out—even to be present at such a council—is extraordinary.

What was Pocahontas doing? A new theory of what we see in the blink of an eye proposes that those who intuit may have an almost unerring take on even a complex individual. As a girl who had been raised to trust her discernment in the agricultural sphere of the women, Pocahontas may have cast her discriminating eye on Smith and been fascinated by what she saw and heard. Throughout the meal, he had told his tales of planets, kingdoms, races, stars, and religions, and these marvelous tales might have impressed her—possibly like those she had heard from her uncle. She may have calculated the threat presented by the storyteller and, deciding that he was harmless, wanted to know more. Here was a man from a foreign place who had a lot to say on just about everything. She apparently implored her father and then made a scene, insisting perhaps in the manner of a willful child demanding satisfaction.

> And being ready with their clubs to beate out his braines, Pocahontas the Kings dearest daughter, when no intreaty could pravaile, got his head in her armes, and laid her owne upon his to save him from death: whereat the Emperour was contented he should live to make him hatchets, and her bells, beads, and copper....

This single sentence is the root of all the debate among the romantics, whether cynical or credulous. It is yet another odd note in Smith's amateur earnestness that this is how he portrays the meeting between himself and Pocahontas. How people meet is important, for that moment can set the pattern for their ensuing relationship. Beyond Smith's skill as a writer, we can see here just on how many levels this scene works. As Smith sat up, facing a new direction in his life, the analogy of the compass comes into play: he was now facing her and his life would take a new direction, following her lead. Taken in an allegorical and spiritual reading, the moment places New World before Old, the vulnerable girl against the broken

veteran, and imbues native spirit into Smith's rebirth. Although Smith and Pocahontas both revolve slowly, turning one round another onto a new path in life, they would remain companions not lovers, adjacent and relational, even special, but never, finally, as one. Their connection, though complete, would always be parallel. On another level, Smith just may well have seen a small, naked girl whose head was shaved and whose chin and jaw line were lively with tattoos. And she may have seen a face with hair and crinkly eyes.

Taking Smith's written words as fact, some scholars believe the ceremony happened, averring to its likelihood as a scene of symbolic adoption, an induction in which his old self was killed, and his sponsor brought his new self into the tribe. Pocahontas may have played that role for Smith, for in the months to come she certainly paid attention to his well-being, and that of his peers, with an interest we would associate with sponsorship. If so, she could not have been a child, but had to have been seen as a young woman, to play a ceremonial role in his adoption. Other scholars doubt there was any ritual at all, that Smith made it up for dramatic effect. We will never know the truth behind the story, and accidents and other miscues doubtless drive more history than all the best-laid plans of scholars.

The story continues that once Smith was spared, he became the slave of Pocahontas, once again the possession of an independent royal. Smith does not write of the following few days during which he belonged to her, but he might have seen in her a child as curious as he had been, and for whom the act of learning would become an obsession as fun and distracting as it been for him. For teacher and student, the days might have passed with a pleasing intensity, strange and intimate. Pocahontas may have restored him to himself, allowing him to rediscover that which he had loved; in sharing this side of him with her, he may have offered her a new world. The intensity of his friendship, from his side, reflected a desperate confidence in his new ally and protector, when he still felt vulnerable to execution.

While all of that is speculation, of course, what remains beyond question is that, as an observant man, Smith did notice that all of the Indians who ate also worked—even the paramount chief made his own clothes. The Indians had a meritocracy, and though it was rough, and the women did most of the labor, it worked better than what the English were doing on the swampy island in the James River.

After a few days went by, Powhatan came to Smith, who was in a hut outside town. He was fierce and painted black, as were his courtiers. He announced that Smith was now the werowance of his own tribe, the Capahowasick, and that he would love Smith as he did his own son, and singled out Nantaquoud for the honor of comparison. Smith had been reborn and given a new direction on the coordinates of his adoptive people. But he had done the same thing, without realizing it, with the chief's favorite daughter. Their mutual influence on each other would guide both cultures in the years ahead and in all the havoc to follow.

What had transpired was a secular miracle. Smith was made a member of a new nation, and while he would retain his separate identity, he would also merge toward a new identity, so much so that by the end of his two years in Virginia, other colonials would accuse him of having gone too native. Here in play is the melding of American immigration today in which we expect those of other nations to retain a core of native individuality though they pursue individualism here under a new name. To fuse these layers is an alloy expressly American, the Powhatan the first to practice this in our shared history, and Smith its first reborn national. The fact that he feared for his life seared it into story form, galvanizing its inner truth, like that of a parable, for those who could decode its meaning. There is no small irony that his first place in this new society was that of a slave. And it is no small accident, either, that in his first observations, he noticed not the hierarchy but the meritocracy of the tribe.

SHE WAS A PRINCESS ON A VISIT TO THE NEW TRIBE IN HER

FATHER'S CHIEFDOM—AND, AS THE ENGLISH NOTED IN ASTONISHMENT, THE NATURALS TRAVELED THROUGH THEIR DECIDUOUS

METROPOLIS WITHOUT GETTING LOST OR CHECKING DIRECTIONS. THIS WAS HER

WORLD, AFTER ALL, AND ONE IN WHICH SHE MOVED WITH

UNARMED IMPUNITY, FEARLESS OF PURSUING HER CURIOSITY.

5

Sunrise cast a soft luster across the January sky.

Smith and a small group of Indians walked beneath bands of pearl gray as they made their way from the capital town to the Pamunkey River; the Indians were escorting Smith back to his island fort. It was the fourth day after Smith's adoption into the Powhatan Nation and his anointment as chief of the Capahowasick country, where Powhatan would feed his men, and they would provide him with hatchets and copper—a deal Smith accepted and ignored. A high-pressure arctic air mass had descended, freezing the river into slush for hundreds of yards out; in no more than loincloths, the Indians broke the ice and slush to push the canoes into the flowing channel. (Years later, Smith would recall that in England they would not subject a dog or horse to such brutal cold, but the Powhatan men bore it stoically. Smith's amazement at their resiliency is a theme in his writings. Even so, his observation was yet another dour English appraisal of this landscape: England may be damp and cold in the winter, but this littoral empire is a harsh and uninhabitable waste, with extreme temperatures that are insuperable. Like the Spanish before them, the English should leave.) No one spoke. The deals were behind them. His relationship with Pocahontas, the child who kept him alive for herself, would become a founding American myth.

The compass, which Smith had given Opechancanough, remained with Chief Powhatan; it had changed the direction of all their lives. Smith and Powhatan had started down a long path of mutual obsession, and both would follow their obsessions to their destruction. Powhatan would follow his to the point of allowing his daughter to marry an Englishman, beyond which ceremony his chiefdom would come to a premature end. And Smith would follow his to become the first colonial addicted to a new high: the art of the deal. Without one another, neither of these two ends would have occurred—and Jamestown would likely have slipped out of sight without any more consequence than the lost colony of Roanoke.

By now, Smith had begun to be enthralled by his own cleverness. At one point in his captivity he had asked to communicate with his men in the fort, allegedly to prevent retaliatory acts of aggression because of his captivity. The Indians understood his meaning well. It was their practice to make another chief a slave to incite his men into a suicidal attempt to rescue him from the humiliation. When Smith made his appeal, they complied quickly—though he would never know why. He wrote his note on a piece of paper and they took it to the fort. The written instructions said to give the Indians the items listed, and to prepare for an attack. The Indians were astonished at Smith's magical powers. Somehow, he had made this thing—a piece of paper—talk. When Smith saw what he could do with his opponents, the surge of power made him feel omnipotent—mixed with his constant fear, this elixir was a psychological cocktail born of a dream and a nightmare.

Smith imperiously believed he had the upper hand. The Indians might have the numbers and the food, but he had an advantage. Once he realized he could play the Indians, he became addicted to cutting a deal that he could boast about—how he had tricked,

bullied, or robbed the locals of hundreds of bushels of corn for a piece of copper. Smith wanted to be feared and respected. Powhatan understood that esteem between equals. The two leaders respected that about each other, saw it, liked it. It made for good business. In the beginning, that psychological edge kept the colonials alive. But it wasn't long until the art of the deal that he had cultivated seduced him into becoming someone almost unrecognizable.

Before he returned to England in 1609, Smith's reputation would overspread the region. For the villages he would burn and the people he would extort, and leave starving and weeping, he might be seen as a man who had fallen away from the man he had been eighteen months earlier. He would transmogrify first into an outlaw, and finally—with the English desperate to kill him before he could endanger them further—into someone even he despised: a terrorist to the Indians and a tyrant to his men. Yet, if there was never a night of the soul when he saw the horror, he nevertheless put himself before us as a man. To this day he stands in print, always in the literary public stocks for all to judge. Scholars egg and pelt him routinely now.

But those eighteen months of turmoil were well ahead of Smith and his Indian escort on the day they left Werowocomoco. After a twenty-mile journey that involved canoeing a mile and a half across the Pamunkey, then hiking miles through the woods in the pain of January cold, they arrived at the jagged fort of palisades in the snow. The gates creaked back disclosing a scene of mud, frost, filth, and fire. The stench of feces and urine hung in the air. The fort's inhabitants had given up leaving the enclosure, even to answer the call of nature, because the locals would shoot them with arrows. What faced Smith now was an open latrine, frozen or steaming; the dead lay stacked like cordwood. A disheveled group of men and boys, stooped in pain, thinned out to nothing, shuffled out of the various hovels to greet him. Not a slum in London presented faces so ravaged with hunger.

No one could believe Smith was alive; amid their own dying, the remaining few dozen men from the original landing party had given Smith up for dead. Especially after the barge and its reduced

crew had returned almost two months before with stories of finding Robinson and Emry killed and of hearing George Cassen's horrifying death screams. Smith saw in the seamed and sunken faces around him the descent of death—an acquiescence of the dying, when they fail to see how deeply they stand in their graves, though they speak and walk as the living. Smith came full about and faced Rawhunt, one of Powhatan's bravest and most trusted warriors and the leader of Smith's escort—and the same man who first told Powhatan about the foreigners. It was time for Smith to fulfill his obligation to Powhatan.

As a condition of his release, Smith had promised Powhatan a pair of cannons. All Powhatan's men would have to do is take them home. Smith swung his hand about to indicate a pair of demiculverns. Each one weighed three thousand pounds. All yours, he magnanimously said to Rawhunt; take them with you. When the Indians could not move the cannon, Smith crowed with subdued humor—not only had he managed to secure his release but he had cheated them in the deal, as well. The trickster had done it again, and the edge was sweet. To savor his taste for humiliation, though, he had one cannon fired on a tree. Giant branches fell with a roar of breaking ice. The Indians ran. Rawhunt and his men looked back unsatisfied, and slipped back into the snowy thickets.

Smith's pleasure did not last. Rebellion was afoot at the fort: The men were preparing to leave. Had he returned a day or so later, he would have found the colony abandoned. They weren't going to stay here and die. Of the hundred plus men who had come to Virginia, only thirty-eight survived to argue with Smith that day. Smith turned one of the cannon on the *Discovery*, the lone ship at anchor since Newport had taken the *Godspeed* and *Susan Constant*, yelling that he would sink it into the James, if one man tried to leave.

President Ratcliffe spoke up: Arrest Smith.

The charge was taken from the Bible's book of Leviticus. As he had gotten both Robinson and Emry killed, he should die—by hanging the next day.

The men chained Smith. Then they descended on the corn and venison that Rawhunt and his men had brought to keep them alive.

A few days later, the fort burned to the ground.

In the days and weeks following Smith's departure, life in Werowocomoco returned to normal—even for Pocahontas, although it is tempting to imagine her thinking about Smith. She rose each morning from her bedding of raccoon skins, built atop a bunk running the length of a longhouse, to her life as a child among children in the town. Powhatan granaries were full of corn, so there was corn to grind, bread to make, oysters to collect, and lovely beads of amber—the sizzling rain of the ancient meteor strike—to string into necklaces for use in trade.

One day, however, Pocahontas's life changed

irrevocably: Powhatan sent for her. About six weeks had passed since Powhatan's men had returned without the cannons. Powhatan was not happy about being tricked by Smith; but the Englishmen were now a colony inside his domain and under his protection, and whether they knew this or not, that obligated them to receive royal visits. Powhatan wanted to know how they were faring; a scout had reported that they appeared to be dying. He decided to send Pocahontas as his emissary to the fort; a few warriors would accompany her with gifts of food. He wanted her to find the chief and talk to him, look around, and return with lots of stories. As a girl full of ideas and curiosity, and talkative, she only had to go and later tell her father what she had seen, with no other instruction necessary. Whether this mission was intended as one of compassion or espionage, we will never know, but the ends are not mutually exclusive.

A few days later, Smith felt a sense of relief like joy. He stood atop the palisade, gripping the sharp posts. An approaching party of people had stepped out of the woods: the chief's daughter was

leading a train of men, each one shouldering a parcel of what had to be venison and corn. He gave a shout to open the gate—and something of a cheer of huzzahs went up from the men. They were at work, rebuilding the entire fort.

For Smith, this meant the trickster had escaped one more time. He was keeping count: so far, the score was three attempts by the Indians, and three attempts by the English. When Ratcliffe had arrested him a few weeks earlier, he had sat all day expecting to die at the hands of his own men, compounding his fury and impotence over the injustice. But when the time had come for his execution, the sails of the *John and Francis* appeared. Captain Christopher Newport finally had returned, with sixty new settlers and supplies, after being gone more than eight months. This sort of happy coincidence often makes critics groan, but somehow those who dismiss the Pocahontas story never latch onto this turning point, in which Smith was spared yet again—and with a timing that was just as convenient and romantic. Newport entered the fort, listened to the men's tales of the past months, and, taking command, ordered Ratcliffe to set Smith free. Like a **deus ex machina** of Greek tragedy, he restored order and righted wrongs—the overlay of myth and life. As for the malfeasant Wingfield, the fat little offender waddled onto the next ship home and sailed into near oblivion, remembered for his gluttony, his atrocious indifference to his men's lives, and his obsession with killing John Smith.

Wingfield exemplifies a dynamic that stands in opposition to the Indian way—and which reveals a subtle misunderstanding of Powhatan's intentions toward the colony. The misunderstanding revolved around food, power, and wealth. The

English measured wealth in the acquisition of goods and the ensuing political power that flowed from such a gravitational mass. For the Indians wealth was demonstrated not by its acquisition alone but by its continual redistribution as food to those in need. For the "naturals," power, or at least leverage, flowed from feeding those who could not feed themselves—like the English. And it was not a matter of hospitality alone—it was Powhatan's political acknowledgment that the wretches in the swamp required his paternal compassion to survive; and men without women were the poorest men of all. He had made John Smith, and by extension his companions, part of the Powhatan chiefdom, and would regard them as such, providing them with food. As the spiritual embodiment of his people, Powhatan was their provider as well, and when he placed colonial survival on a plane equal to his own peoples, the adoption was complete and profound. The ceremony that began with Smith now extended to them all. And as the other tribes paid him tribute in corn and venison, skins and copper, this new tribe would pay him tribute in copper and weapons—that was the political order of his nation.

The English, meanwhile, interpreted Powhatan's gifts of food as a kind of benevolence rather than an expression of political power and inclusion in the chiefdom. In this enclave, and later in America, power would be demonstrated not by giving food away, but by the grand acquisition of European fancies on baronial plantations built on the backs of slaves. That expansive iniquity looming just ahead of Jamestown can be traced all the way back to its first example in Wingfield and his starving men, the leader who belabored them to find gold, then stole their rations and grew fat.

Smith, in taking the food back and redistributing it fairly among the men, had become powerful for a time—in the Indian manner. Just as the Indians had cared for him—a generosity he would tell others about the rest of his life, unaware that the benevolence flowed from the deal he had struck with Powhatan, in which he had been adopted—so he cared for his own men. In a curious way, what followed next was deeply natural, yet completely contrary to the English culture of the colony up until then. Smith may have imported economic examples from the Indians, but he also unknowingly imported psychological models of how a life might be richly lived when it is "natural." With Newport's return and subsequent ascendancy to power, Smith garnered a wealth of esteem. He again became popular with the men; his visible and furious concern for their lives elevated him in their eyes. Weeks later, when Pocahontas arrived from the capital with gifts of food, the men of the fort further esteemed Smith, somehow crediting him for the Indians' generosity.

Smith was deeply thankful that mild March day.

He yelled down for his men to open the gates. Pocahontas walked into the fort in front of the food-laden men and soon made herself unforgettable. The boys stared at the little girl: she ran about and played with them, and showed them a trick, which they had never seen before—turning cartwheels. They gaped, not only at this stunt, but also at her nakedness, as she went fanning by, feet over hands, suggesting she was still a child. As the game wore out and the boys drifted off, she searched for the man who had visited her town. She wanted to understand him better and the things that he said.

While Smith was her slave, she had taught him a few words and phrases of her language, adding to the collection that he had begun compiling. From his earliest days of captivity in fall 1607 until he returned to England, Smith amassed a dictionary of some 200 words of the Algonquin dialect, windows on an ancient world. Other colonials also would transcribe their language, and they would disagree with a few of his definitions, but his was the first attempt, and another reflection of his intellectual curiosity— one that he enjoyed sharing with the child who liked to visit him at the fort. Their conversations raise the invariable question of how much history has sprung from a desire to talk to someone

new. As only a sop to boredom, the answer may be: all of it.

Smith's notes on the Algonquin language reveal the lines of stress and peace between him, the Indian men, and Pocahontas. While many of his entries relate matters of business—numbers, for instance—others relate phrases hot with controversy—You lie! I don't lie! His phrases outline various relationships— community born of business, hostility between men—but real affection toward only one person: Pocahontas. Because she was only a child, she may have been the one person with whom he felt entirely safe. She appreciated him. He could relax and be himself with her. His dictionary includes a keystone sentence that carries enormous weight:

> " *Kekaten pokahontas patiaquagh ningh tanks manotyens neer movchick rawrenock audowgh*—Bid Pokahontas bring hither two little Baskets, and I wil give her white beads to make her a chaine. "

In the world that blooms behind this line, we can glimpse an avuncular tenderness, all the more telling because he recorded so few—and if the other sentences had an audience in London, for men and business and war, then why would he bother to record this one about some random child? This sentence is the only one that shows him giving for pleasure, not gain. His inclusion of the line in the dictionary is a tacit confession to the effect she had on him.

Pocahontas and her retinue did not stay long at the fort, but her interest was piqued. In the months that followed, she frequently visited the fort and Smith, and often by herself. In our time of overprotective parents and suburban suffocation inside sealed environments, it is astonishing to think of a ten-year-old girl having the wherewithal to take a canoe across a river, hike for miles through the woods, cross a few streams, and wind up twenty miles later at a fort full of strangers, where she wants to play; yet clearly this little girl did—several colonial accounts note her presence.

In truth, Pocahontas had little to fear: she was a precocious little girl on a visit to the new tribe in her father's chiefdom and, as the English noted in astonishment, the naturals traveled throughout their deciduous metropolis without getting lost or checking directions, with the same ease the English knew in their home towns. This was her world, after all, and she moved with unarmed impunity, fearless of pursuing her curiosity about Smith.

Whether Pocahontas came to feed them, to find out how they were doing,

or to pique her interest in Smith becomes important. At this innocent juncture, when she is maturing, tolerance for this foreign tribe animates her afternoons. If her later leniency for Rolfe began with Smith, then her curiosity about the Smith may have grown into an infatuation—not because they were lovers, but because they were not. She left no account and we may assume too much, but her forays to the fort represent a playfulness that speaks of confidence and affection.

What is most important is not whether she adored Smith, but how the mutual affection between them redirected their sympathies, and subsequently changed the visible course of their lives. Had she been less interested, had he been more obnoxious, had they simply ignored each other, there is no reason to think Jamestown would have become a colony of consequence. On such a slender pinion a lot of weight slowly came to balance.

At some point, their friendship led them to step over a line into a new world and they could not go back to being who they had been before. This new world was layered and nuanced. For them both there was likely a certain rejuvenating effect of their talking; he liked having the girl there; she was amusing and bossed the boys around; and she liked learning about the things he had seen.

Studies of male and female conversation patterns reveal wide discrepancies—not only in subject matter and depth and purpose of conversation, but also of the dynamic of thought. While women emphasize feelings and associations, men focus on facts. Women speak of internal stresses on the social fabric, and explore conclusions on how to fix them—literally within, yet outside the hearing of the males—intending in this way to keep society together and reaffirm the group's inherent values. Men, finding this tedious, denounce it as gossip. They find relevancy in the exterior of things; they point to the perimeter of the group's life: they want to know the facts they need to go right now—by getting something, or someone.

Although they spoke from their different genders, John Smith and Pocahontas likely conversed with some effort to translate and then with more confidence. For while Smith went to the forefront as a leader of men, driving his men, executing jobs and chores, accumulating in his journals thousands of facts about the naturals, the manner of his thinking was nevertheless not male, but female. Strachey and Percy, other colonial writers, left linear accounts that reflect both their superior educations and conventional masculine thinking. Smith's writings reflect free-associational thinking— though he listed lots of facts, he wrote by mood and image. He may have conversed, then, in a way that Pocahontas—and other women—would have been able to hear well, since their inner ears were attuned to making associations. This indirect and nuanced way in which Smith and Pocahontas could think together as one person, and share that thinking, brought the two of them into harmony and deepened their conversation into connection. Some call this parity; some call it soul mates.

The ramifications were serious for them both. In a time when Shakespeare was creating the drama of individual human psychology, Smith was living out that drama in the Virginia woods; it is no coincidence that Smith's was the first autobiography, and that it appeared in the shadows of the high Renaissance. The colonials were always against him: they lived in fear that his ruthlessness would cause the Indians to kill them; he was resented for reaching beyond

his commoner status. Smith was the first to realize the self in the colonial community, and he published his books, asserting his value as an individual.

If the stakes were life or death for Smith, they were higher still for Pocahontas because they would involve all whom she loved. Her fixation with Smith raises a question on point about what her friendship with Smith did for her, and whether it directly elicited a new knowledge of the self. Was that the essence of Smith's appeal? Did he lead her into a new and fascinating self-awareness, at least of how far away everything else was, and by extension how far she was from all of it, and from a different way of life, a different kind of self? Was there something essentially troubling yet exhilarating that came to her in all those talks with him? As Smith envisioned a new self in the New World, did she envision a new self somewhere else? There is no way to know, but the tensions between the group and the individual affected them both.

The self as a vaunted entity was only starting its celebrated renaissance in Europe. In traditional communities, like those of the Powhatan and the English, the individual was often submerged inside the group. Not all love is about making love, of course, and not all lovers leave the conversation for the bed. To think of them too narrowly, then, we may well miss the visible if subtle influence of endearing affection.

Smith may have given her a seminal new self and with it a growing awareness of a life within her to be born outside the community. In a few years, that self-awareness would grow into an entirely new woman, no longer a playful child but an assertive adult. Their influence was reciprocal. Just as it is not a coincidence that Smith is credited with writing the first autobiography, it is not a coincidence that she may have been the first woman to stand up to the paramount chief, her people by extension, and to survive.

This tension between the self and the community still drives conflicts today, expressed most aptly in the strain between younger generations leaving the farm behind for the city and new identities and older generations that see in this exodus the erosion of traditional values. Even the Declaration of Independence hits on this founding tension when Thomas Jefferson posits "we the people" alongside the "pursuit of happiness," as though they were the same. For Smith, the end of his pursuits would not be happy, and for Pocahontas they would lead to a final and tragic estrangement from her father.

All of that was years ahead of them. For now, Pocahontas was just a girl and becoming infatuated with the man at the fort. As the months passed, the colonials saw how fixed Pocahontas was on Smith; they teased Smith about her—which annoyed him. Smith did not like being the butt of jokes; he was too sensitive, his self-esteem too brittle. However, he never turned Pocahontas away when she came calling with food for him and his men. Smith was a reflexive speaker; he just needed an audience and a reason. An autodidact, explorer, and writer, he would talk to her—and the worlds he opened up in her imagination were not just those of other places, but of those already inside her. There may have been another form of stimulation, as well—the exact flash of eyes and curl of smile that entices one closer to someone. Once looks draw a person in, that person is then close enough to inhale a suite of pheromones.

Such a comprehensive stimulation writes neural pathways that are scored by intense emotion. This chemistry cannot be taken lightly or descriptively, for it can fuse people. New studies in biochemistry show how passion can fit the same chemical profile of obsessive-compulsive disorders. When you love someone, this part of the brain ignites, and though a loved one may leave you in body, that person will be with you always in spirit—in your heart and in the architecture of your mind.

As Pocahontas's self-possession and confidence grew into independence and individuality, her being with Smith may have seemed to her the natural fulfillment of this heady maturation. To the extent that Smith still saw her as a child, and refused her, she might think of him more and more often, until he seemed always present in her imagination at home, during meals: what he had said one time, why he had given her that look, and what it would be like to *be* with him. She

went to see him, and her fascination seems to have grown into a crush and deepened into longing. In this way, her maturing sense of self led her to the turning points that would end in catastrophe for her father and her people. The two of them maintained a delicate equilibrium, close without colliding, always allies without regard for the relations between the English and the Indians.

One day something went wrong. Shouting broke out among the men and the Indians. The naturals were deft at stealing any object, often with nearly invisible stealth. Colonials wrote that, even as a warrior faced you in conversation, he might use his toes to slip something off the ground and into his hand. Once caught, he would claim it had been his all along, and fight to keep it. It was just such a quarrel that Smith interrupted: six Indians were caught. Smith ordered his men to fire volleys of shot. The Indians were convinced that their fellows were killed, and confessed to stealing the weapons so they could turn them over to Powhatan.

By now, a lot had changed between the English and the Powhatan. It was almost summertime, and at Smith's direction, the men were digging freshwater wells away from the river. Smith and Newport had met with Powhatan, and Smith had seen his superior officer offer up expensive copper in exchange for just a few bushels of corn. Smith had countered by giving blue glass beads to the children, but refusing to give them to Powhatan, who soon wanted them inordinately. The Venetian blue glass, pale as noon, was mesmerizing for those who knew only the familiar meteoric amber. At the end of the deal, Smith walked away with hundreds of bushels for a handful of beads, compared to Newport's ten for copper. Smith had learned something about dealing with the Indians that Newport had not—that you had to appear strong, or indifferent. Any sign of niceness or wanting to be liked was seen as weakness, and even worse, invited contempt and betrayal. It was the colonial men's niceness at the fort, he believed, that had brought on the stealing.

Smith decided to kill the six Paspahegh men. It would reestablish fear and respect. None of the English disagreed. Although many of the men had thought him too harsh in the past, they had also seen several of their own killed, pierced through with the arrows of men whose chiefs did not always obey Powhatan or observe his deals, even though they were in the coalition. Smith sent a man to Powhatan to tell him that six of his warriors would be executed and why.

Powhatan then made an extraordinary move.
He sent a party of men to meet with Smith. When they reached the fort, Rawhunt spoke for Powhatan, but he was unable to convince Smith. Then the chief's favorite daughter, Pocahontas, walked out from behind the men. Until then, she had been aloof. Opechancanough sent men to ask him to spare the lives of two friends of his; families also arrived, begging Smith for mercy. All Smith would do, though, was order them tied to a tree to be shot. In all of this posturing, the remarkable girl appeared indifferent, in the same manner of her father, when he dealt with Smith.

The English were stunned. Why did Powhatan send a child—a girl, no less; and why Pocahontas? Was his favorite daughter expendable? Did Powhatan think she would be more persuasive than Rawhunt? Or did she symbolize an uncompromising gesture of trust from Powhatan? Even if sending a daughter was customary, why had he sent *this* daughter?

Pocahontas reasoned with Smith quietly and asked him to relent.

Smith fumed but he listened. And then, this man who was proud of his fearsome reputation, who had won the colonials' lives many times with his deals among various tribes, who was on the high of getting a lot for nothing, capitulated to the child. Colonial accounts other than Smith's attest to this extraordinary moment. Smith gave in. He later wrote that he said to Pocahontas and to his men just this: that only to this girl would he ever deliver these men alive. No one, not even Powhatan himself, could have convinced him to let them go. Only *she* could have taken them out of the fort alive, and that is how the six Paspaheghs left that day, under the protection of Pocahontas.

What had she said to convince him? No dialogue is recorded of the negotiation, but one thing is clear. Smith identifies her for the first time in *A True Relation*, and describes her as the "nonpareil" of her people. The common coin of that exchange was life for life. She wanted the lives of those men, and Smith felt obligated to recognize a debt. His sense of honor demanded that he honor a life for a life.

But how narrowly or broadly conceived was that debt, of life for a life? If the debt he owed was to her father alone for sparing his life, then Rawhunt should have won the negotiation, but didn't. If the debt was owed because the English had received so much food, then once again her place—as a child and a girl—would be all wrong for the world of politics in which men would negotiate exclusively with other men. Powhatan's sending of his daughter, then, is strange—her presence speaks to something that Smith had not yet been man enough to admit to his fellow Englishmen. He might not have been completely straight with them. Just as his captivity with the Turks hints at something heinous happening to him, which he did not write about, something else might have happened to him in captivity with the

Powhatan that he did not mention, either. He did not like being held up for ridicule, and Pocahontas was already a sore spot for him. But such a secret might also explain why Pocahontas hung around so much.

Smith's words indicate that his sense of debt was to the girl, to Pocahontas exclusively, and to no one else: she was the one person to whom he owed a debt in this exact exchange of life for life. In this declaration, he gave in defiantly, saying that all other negotiators would have failed; his words denote a favor repaid out of consideration alone, nothing else—and certainly not justice. Powhatan had surmised this about Smith and had sent Pocahontas there to collect. Powhatan, ever the thoughtful politician, knew the man he had dealt with, and of the fascination his daughter enjoyed for him. He had calculated that Smith would acknowledge the debt, recognize her sincere appeal and leverage over him, and that he would spare the men, just as Smith himself had been spared. That

was not all. With her periodic arrivals with food and conversation, wit, play, and charm, she was the natural person to find that chink in his armor-plated arrogance and prick his conscience. And by then, they all owed Powhatan their lives anyway—as her presence alone would remind him.

And so Smith let the Paspaheghs go. The scene points to a founding event between Smith and Pocahontas and a respect that they shared and which profoundly affected them. Other scenes of similar poignancy would make them alive to each other, epiphanies that played out from an unknowable something between them, which lives on enigmatically. As if he were never fully able to thank her, he credited her for obvious things like saving the colony, but also for more subtle incidents like the one above, when she seems to have restored him to himself. He understood this darkly when he looked back and wrote about the child who came one day and taught him there was more to the deal than art.

THIS TIME HE WAS ON ONE OF HIS GREAT, UNALLOYED

ADVENTURES

TO LIMN THE ELEVEN THOUSAND MILES OF THE SHORELINE OF THE

CHESAPEAKE BAY, FOLLOWING

THE HEROIC IMPERATIVE

OF HIS TIME.

By spring, brimming with insight and drama, Smith set quill to paper and wrote an account of the settlement's first arduous year in Virginia. The missive was directed to his London superiors of the Virginia Company. It was later published, probably in late fall 1608, without Smith's knowledge, under the title *A True Relation of Occurrences and Accidents in Virginia*. His descriptions of this strange new world and its native peoples entertain and intrigue any reader, then and now.

In a mixture of journalism, ethnography, and personal adventure, Smith relates the hard life in the colony from his viewpoint, on everything from their arrival onward. While his later books replay many of the same scenes with more detail and drama, this letter is often seen as the one so close to the events, and so wanting in self-aggrandizement, that scholars often look upon it as the one most credible by his hand. Even so, hooks remain for the larger stories later on—as in his reference to the "nonpareil" of the Powhatan people, meaning a girl more brilliant and beautiful than all others, who is later identified as Pocahontas in that scene about the return of the native men. While the *True Relation* is famous for what it reveals, it is infamous for what it does not say, making him the first great unreliable narrator of American history.

Smith, it turns out, omitted quite a few events, which forms a meaningful pattern. Among other things, he fails to mention that he was charged with mutiny, that gallows were built for him, that he sued Wingfield for libel and won, that the Powhatan wanted to kill him on three separate occasions. Most notorious though, the missive does not mention that Pocahontas saved his life when he was captured by the Powhatan. As such, the controversy over the role of Pocahontas in the Jamestown story begins with this account. Some 250 years later, his first critic, Henry Adams, would launch the argument that this omission indicates that Smith later made up the story to make himself look good.

This is a plausible theory; however, some scholars will point out that he leaves out everything of a *personal* nature, writing instead a *professional* account of the colony and the colonists. Smith was a lead agent of the Virginia Company; it was important to him that his intended audience see him as a professional. The series of omitted episodes would not have portrayed him as a consummate professional, rather as a willful man whose enemies thought he endangered the colony. Had Smith admitted to these failures, the executives of the Virginia Company would have called him back to London. But he could not go, not yet—not before he had a chance to succeed at something, here in Virginia.

Up until this time, the success or esteem enjoyed by other men who had come to the New World had eluded Smith. He was not a royal favorite, as the swashbuckling Sir Walter Raleigh was to Queen Elizabeth; nor was he a genocidal terrorist like Hernan Cortés, whose actions were known the breadth of the New World and had horrified non-Catholic Europe. Success in coin and esteem was the inner and personal frontier that he came here to explore—as immigrants still do today. Smith could not afford to be seen as an ineffective leader.

Like many commanders on a losing front, Smith had to look

good. It is only natural that he fell into a cover-up by following the formula of a professional letter. Although he relates how his men and others were killed, the want of anything negative about himself makes him look brilliant by default. He also relishes how he simply charms Chief Powhatan, who is delighted to meet him. He never admits to fear or failure; he brags of his exploits. He does not mention the mutiny or Pocahontas saving his life. For anyone who wants to call him a liar, there it is: lies of omission. Other accounts may seem biased, mistaken, or argumentative—but, finally, open to interpretation.

What mattered to Smith in his accounting of the settlement's first year is only the deed of historic consequence—one measured by male standards. Emotions and feelings—the inner life, along with the lives of women and children, are of no importance—in the male sphere.

Outside the little room where he composed his letter, outside its positive scope, life in the fort was not going well. By the summer of 1608, the Jamestown story has many players and plots, attempted coups and counterattacks; its schemes resemble the impossibly branching creeks of the tidewater region where it all happened. The chronology is dense, complex, and frustrating, with many people on all sides of the English factions, writing contradictory accounts. To place more emphasis on Pocahontas, or even Smith, is essentially a distortion—yet, they, along with Powhatan, Opechancanough, and eventually John Rolfe, form a psychological spine to the Jamestown story. While other people are important to history, these players are crucial to identity formation—nerves that still wire and fire the way we think. If we removed them, the others would form an amorphous series of blunders and murders without any memorable

dynamic, and the tragedy would be subsumed in the marshes.

A few weeks after penning his report, Smith lay dying—or so he believed. His shoulder had swelled with poison and the agony was unendurable. Smith and a few men had been sloshing about in the river trying to catch the abundant fish in frying pans, but when that didn't work, they grabbed their swords and thrust them into the water, attempting to spear the fish. Sometime amid this comedy, an eerie creature of the sea with a flat body like a shovel blade, which none of them had seen before, came flailing out on Smith's sword, whipped about, and stung him on the arm with its toxin-filled tail. The last man to lose control if possible, Smith gave orders for the men to dig his grave and to read his last rites over him. He was just being practical but also, perhaps, living out the melodrama of his traumatized psyche. Although he lay down to die, by nightfall he was up for dinner. A man with a taste for revenge and credit both, he ate the stingray, and then named the place Stingray Isle.

Smith was in the middle of a great, unalloyed adventure to limn the eleven thousand miles of shoreline of the Chesapeake Bay, following the heroic imperative of his time. In the summer of 1608, Smith spent three months crisscrossing the bay and sailing far up its major tributaries. At one point, Smith sailed to a halt along the Potomac River, and enjoyed the view of shimmering light over the marshlands—a swampy area on which eventually a new nation's capital, Washington, D.C., would rise and expand. Smith had come to the end of his personal quest: he had accomplished all he had hoped. His map and recognizance of the indigenous nations would place him among the great explorers; fame and respect would be his upon his return both to the colony and to England.

On his return downriver, Smith launched a game of psychological warfare against the Indians. Until then, he had antagonized only Powhatan and the tribes of his nation, but now he began spreading his reputation wider, into the tribal nations surrounding the Powhatan coalition. The propaganda of his ferocity had two components, one real and the other imaginary.

The real was terrifying.

One day, in their travels along the bay, a group of Indians had hailed the English to come ashore for a feast. Smith detected an ambush—he does not give the reasons why in his later accounts—and ordered his men to open fire, leaving men and women sprawled on the ground. When the men went ashore, they found blood everywhere and an abandoned village. Now that Smith and his men had proved their dominance, they left beads, copper, and eyeglasses, to indicate their friendliness. The Indians who had fled in terror returned and traded peacefully. Smith had set an example: violence and then peace equals fair trade. On behalf of the Virginia Company, he left new bloody prints in American business history. These were the facts that lent weight to his great lie about the Massawomeck. Witnesses to one event made the other seem true.

The Massawomeck falsehood grew out of an encounter that Smith had with a tribe near the confluence of the bay and the Potomac. The tribe refused to trade with Smith and then further annoyed him by refusing to take him upriver to meet with the Massawomeck. Renowned as a fierce tribe, members of the Iroquois coalition, and Powhatan's antagonists, the Massawomeck were terrifying. Smith and his men proceeded upriver anyway, eventually coming across a wandering band of Indians who traded peacefully with them. When Smith returned downriver with his boat heavily ladened, the earlier tribe asked where Smith had gotten the gain. Smith blithely said: the Massawomeck. We fought with them, killed them, and took everything they had.

The news ran through the woods. By the time Smith got back to the fort, he was famous throughout the Powhatan chiefdom for having fought and killed enemies whom Powhatan himself would not engage. Even more startling, the most diligent enemies of the Massawomeck had heard about the slaughter and they wanted to meet with him. They were the "gyant-like" Susquehannock from the north, Powhatan's genuine terrors, renowned for their

gigantic stature and their reputation as cannibals. In his language of the account—having sailed through "limbo" and now meeting "giants"—Smith lights his adventures in the rhetoric of fables. He slyly places his renown into the mouths of giants, thus elevating himself in stature and casting his shadow far and wide. Of all the fascinating tales, he claims that he finally met with representatives of the warring Susquehannock, who feted him with dancing, and gave him gifts, including a seven-pound chain of pearls about his neck and mantles of skins. Smith promised to return in a year and fight the Massawomeck.

Not only was Smith news along the trails and trade routes, but he later managed to work a miracle, as well. Sometime in mid-1609, he helped an Indian captive, imprisoned for stealing, recover from smoke inhalation and burns, and then released him to his brother's care. Taken together, these stories of a man who had bested the enemies of the Powhatan, and then had raised the dead elevated Smith's persona over the forest to a force of near divinity— and, finally, of a scope to rival Chief Powhatan himself.

If one follows Smith's growing reputation too closely, though, one might miss out on the wonders of his reporting. As Smith and his men explored the Potomac and other rivers, they met with people almost unknown to us now. His account brims with names that convey ancient continuity in places like Patawomeck, Cecocawonee, Mayaones, Nacotchtant, and Toags, where the folks traded well with him, with bear and deer meat. They rowed as far as they could up a little river called Quiyough, and then traveled with Indians eight miles to a mine. A brook flowing with "christal-like" water provided locals with a tincture they used as paint, on humans and figurines. The paint made "them looke like Blackmores dusted over with silver," but later analysis in England showed no silver in the mixture.

Smith got glimpses of a vast and tantalizing interior of the continent and heard reports of great lakes and of many other tribes. He found marvels of an ancient character. He uses words in his

account like "giants" and "limbo" that impart not only his overt intentions as a writer, but also the inclinations of his age—to see wonders in the world, and then render them in suitably marvelous terms. Such a rhetorical dimension would surround his Pocahontas story, and undermine it in later centuries. Nevertheless, somewhere beyond his style, what remains most wonderful is the picture he presents of the world outside Powhatan's nation. The tribes and the politics show how insignificant the English still were in the native realm of real politics. Had they been driven out, the psychological damages would have gone with them.

Viewing Tsenacommacoh—the Powhatan chiefdom—from such a fresh perspective, one can see the anachronistic fallacy in presenting Powhatan history in connection with the English alone. A more accurate picture is that the English were just one small group of men inside a nation, the rambling perimeter of which was populated with dozens of tribes in a mosaic of relations and agreements, rich and figured. The tribes, their histories of conflict, their fear, disdain, or ignorance of Powhatan, all convey a fractious complexity. A likely reason Powhatan took no direct action on the English fort, often leaving its inhabitants to die of their own accord or discord, is because his borders were rife with conflict. To the Powhatan, the Englishmen, who could neither feed themselves nor reproduce, having failed to bring women, were of little consequence. Even so, the fear inspired by Smith's terrorism would work on the Powhatan coalition as the stingray toxin had worked on Smith.

After Smith returned in September from his expeditions around the bay, he resumed meeting periodically with Powhatan, something he and other colonial leaders had been doing ever since Smith's return from captivity in January 1608. Their interactions were necessarily strained by the differences in culture. On one occasion, Smith went to visit Powhatan and found the capital town empty. A lone warrior remained to escort him to a new meeting place. When they got to a clearing in the woods, Smith, ever suspicious, pulled

his musket. That was when the Indians came laughing out of the forest, and then fed him and feted him like a royal visitor. They loved to goose him, and they laughed at his startled response—he never disappointed them.

On one visit, in early fall 1608, Smith had an encounter with Pocahontas that catalyzed the rumors they were lovers. The scene is well documented in the accounts of other men then present. Before Powhatan arrived for their meeting, some thirty other young women entertained Smith and his men; Pocahontas, by now eleven or thirteen, was among them. The performance surprised the men: the women cried out from the woods and rushed into the field so violently that Smith and his men grabbed the older Indian men as hostages. No, Pocahontas told him, We are not attacking you—indeed, please kill me, if we hurt you.

They danced for the men,

and Smith especially. They wore skirts made of leaves, indicating their status as women, not children; their bodies were painted red and black and varicolored combinations. The leader wore a headdress of deer horns and a quiver of arrows slung across her back. They left after an hour, only to return later and "solemnly" invite Smith alone into a house, where he later complains in his *General History*, "all these nymphs more tormented him that ever, with crowding, pressing and hanging about him, most tediously crying, *Love you not me? Love you not me?*"

In the morning, the men goaded Smith. That girl loves you, they crowed; you could marry her and inherit the whole kingdom. Smith was furious and told them to stop; it wasn't like that. In the eyes of some scholars, his remark proves that he was aware that the tribe was a matrilineal society—in other words, the next in line for paramount chief were Powhatan's brothers and sisters, not his daughter Pocahontas—and that he was nothing more than a sly and conniving adventurer. It is more likely still that he either could not, or would not, consummate the seduction and

was speaking up for her—at least in print—as would a gentleman, the single calling that he was obsessed with but frustrated from achieving. Most notable in Smith's account of this scene, though, is not what he tells us, but what he does not tell us. Not a word about what went on inside the hut.

A trip wire of anachronistic piety runs through the underbrush here: to address the issue of a relationship between them today is to rouse protective and censorious instincts in people of good will. Were it not for her legendary status, some might even sniff at any discussion of possible intimacy as licentiousness. The fact that many people today are distressed or infuriated over talk of any inappropriate relations between them may give us a hint about why Smith, himself, became furious when his own men began gossiping. What the allegations of sexuality present, then, is not impropriety alone, but the ways in which others will use rumors for leverage—to destroy enemies.

Although what follows is reading between the lines, Pocahontas was not with him that morning and, more telling, it seems that she also stopped coming to visit him at the fort. Smith doesn't say that, but she does vanish from his and other people's accounts. The men, looking at the obvious—the facts and their linear presentation—got the story wrong; that's why they teased him. Smith's fury with his men also implies some distress on his part over what might have happened, and some sense of how he might have wounded her. Her apparent absence that morning, and for a long time to come, does not corroborate the gossip that they were lovers; rather, it does the reverse. It hints at a young woman humiliated by the way she had offered herself, unmistakably this time, and once again had been turned down.

To understand her humanity in this moment of her life, the puritans and zealots will have to let her make her own choices and mistakes outside our mores. In her community, in front of her maidens, when she had made that formal gesture in the style and maturity of the dance, she was not supposed to be rejected. The scene had been prepared, the feast had been enjoyed, and, like a

favored daughter, she had meant to have the man she wanted—but this time it would be on her terms. She may have wanted to become a woman with him, possibly even to marry him, and sexuality for her was not the sin it was for him. In her freedom, without the Christian freight of sin or obligation, an expression of her sexuality may simply have been a natural development for her.

Pocahontas may have been infatuated with him, and many infatuations often reach their full effect to the extent that they are unrealized. It is likely that if her infatuation ran high and hot, it was not because they were lovers but because they were not. Although still young, Pocahontas was closing in on the time when she would marry. Her sisters had married at twelve, thirteen, or fourteen. Each had been selective and had chosen a young warrior who had shown himself a skilled hunter. At the tender age of eleven or thirteen, then, Pocahontas was ready and heady for life. Moreover, according to contemporary accounts, by September 1609, Pocahontas had matured into a fully formed woman with hips and breasts. To continue seeing her as a child, then, is to infantilize her.

The idea of a youthful bride would not have been out of the ordinary for the English. With lives famously nasty, brutish, and short, the English would compensate those harsh realities with early marriage. Smith and the other colonials would have heard the young cry of the heart in the arias of *Romeo and Juliet*, staged at the Globe; Juliet was thirteen, but her youth caused no scandal, and her romantic verse is incandescent. At thirteen, life took one by the hand. Time was briefly yours; you might not reach thirty. In spite of their broadly different cultures, both the English and Indian societies knew of youth in all its passionate intensity; and they knew of early death.

The subject of marriage between Smith and Pocahontas, however, seems never to have been discussed between Smith and Powhatan, giving credence to the story that they were never lovers, this night or any other night. Although sex did not compel marriage for the Powhatan, had they been intimate, Powhatan likely would have precipitated marital conversations as part of all his dealings with

Smith; they had bartered for women before. If we believe that Pocahontas was responsible for Smith's life being saved, which subsequently led to his being adopted by Powhatan, then she and Smith were now sister and brother—anything sexual between them would be incestuous. Her own words reflect this understanding. Many years later, she addressed Smith as father—and father only. And he addressed her as daughter. In conflict with herself and her own cultural mores, she may still have wanted Smith, and it seems that her eagerness to be with him was often frustrated.

From the very beginning, Smith does not brag about conquering Pocahontas, as he did with other women who saved his life. He swears that he did *not* take her, but no one believes him—a perfect reversal. Smith is so clearly outside the confidence of the other men that he cannot find one ally to believe him; he is isolated.

The male group, with its linear thinking, could not fathom the subtleties that only the women would have surmised. Smith was yet again an individual apart from the group. Pocahontas may have attempted a similar distinction by trying to consummate her new status with the English chief. Although they were in some way complicit in their friendship, they were not going to be a couple. She distanced herself physically; he defended her honor. Like two people joined by an essential, unshakable bond, Smith and Pocahontas apparently did this together—in a slow step of retreat.

If Smith was anything, he was difficult. On this occasion, he may have offended her. The sense of value, of self, which he had helped to awaken in her, might have been injured, causing her to wonder: If he thought she was so great, then what was wrong with her? What was wrong with *him*? Was he being a gentleman? Was he distraught by the advances of such a young girl? Smith's tales in *A General History* do not answer these hypothetical questions, but he writes of being "tormented" by the maidens, which captures both the desire and the pain of controlling himself. The torment seems to have gone both ways, and if she never got over him, he never got over her, either.

Smith was twenty-eight the night she danced for him, but he would write of her for years to come, and always with a keen sense of loss. He admired her and memorialized her when others could not see her in the throng or care enough; and though others used her status to create peace, or her celebrity to promote the colony, he focused on her thoughts and feelings—her distress when she was kidnapped, and even her furious impatience with him when they met again later in London. His desire to shield her is poignant for a military man who could show so much contempt for her people. Years after she was gone and slipping away in popular memory, it was John Smith who rescued her—from oblivion, and finally returned a favor he could never thank her for with suitable power.

FOR THE MOMENT. . . SMITH HAD WON.

WARRIORS, "GRIM AS DIVELS,"

REMAINED BEHIND TO GUARD

THE CORN,

7

In September 1608, an inspired Smith returned to

the fort from his expeditions around the bay, and the men elected him as president of the colony. They recognized that his successful dealings with Powhatan and his fearsome reputation were all that were keeping them alive. Smith quickly dispelled the men's goodwill. Although the colonials now had wells, had given up looking for gold, and were trying fruitlessly to make a go of timber and tar, Smith was nevertheless piqued with the lazy gentlemen, who thought everyone else was obligated by class to work and to feed them. He made a startling new decree, drawing his legalistic reference from the Bible. "You must obey this now for a Law, that he that will not worke shall not eate (except by sickness he be disabled) for the labours of thirtie or fortie honest and industrious men shall not be consumed to maintaine an hundred and fiftie idle loyterers." Smith's order may have been derived from the Bible, but he had also imported native ideas across cultural lines. He had lived among the Naturals, and in spite of his fears, had studied their culture, gleaned its underpinnings, and then applied their principles. With this new law—no work, no eat—the combative little captain had become a usurper. In one command, Smith had overthrown the inherited structure of his society.

The uproar was immediate. As the colony's president, he alone could order the changes; he enforced them, no matter how unpopular he became. In time, Smith noted that a curious sense of wellbeing began suffusing the men. He observed a psychological phenomenon similar to the one already enjoyed by the Naturals: with tangible accomplishment comes a rush of satisfaction and esteem that fills the mind, as studies of biochemistry and serotonin levels show. Under Smith's leadership, the English began to build an identity founded on accomplishments, not inheritance or blood. As the colonials grew happier with their newfound competencies, their English style of life began to die out—at least until new settlers arrived much later. Smith sent groups of people to live upriver, anywhere away from the fetid little island, and sent them to live with the Naturals—a tacit recognition that the Indians knew how to live well. The English stopped dying and survived. With some qualifications, the English seem to have enjoyed the stability, routine, and community of the Indian way of life over the artificial obligations of the colony; yet no change is easy. The English would return to form—but not to the fort. One of the ironies is that their new competence gave them the ability to survive outside the fort and up the river—a violation of the primary condition of Smith's original deal with Powhatan.

Accomplishment achieved in the Indian manner endowed in them a new level of confidence and competence. Success told them who they were. To a sharp new degree, they were not English anymore; they were American. The name was not yet in use, but the attitude was, and their letters home reflect a resilient new stubbornness, an attitude of willful disobedience tantamount to rebellion. As new standards based on skill replaced social status as the measure of accomplishment, the roots of a new meritocracy sank into the psychological soil of Jamestown.

This fresh sense of empowerment was the new crop grown out of the Indian example of society—of a natural society, reborn with cross-fertilization. The hybrid of Indian interdependence and English governance catalyzed a new temperament among the colonials, which they would cultivate over the next century into an expansive and, finally, national sense of identity. It is not a coincidence that when the new Americans declared themselves not English, one of the first things that they did was to lose the wig and wool and put on a buckskin shirt—to go "native" sartorially and, in effect, declare their identification with the First Americans and their landscape.

Some of the irony is unfathomable. Smith learns from the Indians and imparts this wisdom to the colony; the colonials benefit enough to begin a new life of practicality, yet, in his absence, they stop pursuing his directives. Seasoned colonials who detested Smith and just-arrived colonials—who want to see his natural improvements disappear and the old English culture restored—are well enough to conspire to kill Smith. Smith learns his examples from a people whom he might one day respect and another day terrorize.

The year 1609 represents a sliding point in the balance of power between the English and the Powhatan. The results of Smith's explorations of the Chesapeake Bay were far more complex and injurious than even he might have imagined. His reputation for ferocity hit its zenith, and the Powhatan were ill-prepared for Smith's brand of psychological warfare. The Powhatan were not innocent in the use of psychology to terrorize their opponents—their constant raids of attrition against the colony were heavily demoralizing—but the results were acute, galvanizing the English around their identity, and encouraging them to return home as soon as possible.

Smith's violence against the tribes, in contrast, presented the Powhatan coalition with a chronic crisis. Smith's brand of warfare was a contaminant that would prove as psychologically viral as any contagion

the Spanish might have brought earlier. It weakened first the coalition, then compelled the tribes' movements within a landscape, and, finally, disrupted their national identity as the Powhatan. Although the Powhatan would display their resiliency for five or six more decades, and Chief Powhatan would act on his political acumen in a striking series of moves, the result was nevertheless catastrophic. In 1609, following a year of persistent invasion and stress, the Powhatan very likely began to suffer from the psychological effects of terrorism—and the master terrorist was John Smith.

As with all the other caveats in this story, we are clearly looking back through four centuries with a modern lens and falling into what might be a narcissistic fallacy—to see others in the past too closely as we see ourselves. Even so, we can look into Powhatan's political moves to gather a sense of the deeper nature of the crisis they were facing in Smith.

Chief Powhatan first threatened, to no avail, the tenuous balance of power between himself and Smith in January 1609. Smith had arrived in Werowocomoco to deal for corn. The negotiations were fraught with the poignancy and the paranoia of two men who trade but cannot trust. Smith later chronicled their exchange in his 1624 *A General History*. The chief opens the negotiations with an eloquent speech heavy with loss.

"'Captaine Smith you may understand, that I, having seen the death of all my people thrice, and not one living of those 3 generations, but my self, I know the difference of peace and warre, better then any in my Countrie. But now I am old, and ere long must die, my brethren, namely Opichapam, Opechankanough, and Kekataugh, my two sisters, and their two daughters, are distinctly each others successours, I wish their experiences no lesse then mine, and your love to them, no less then mine

114

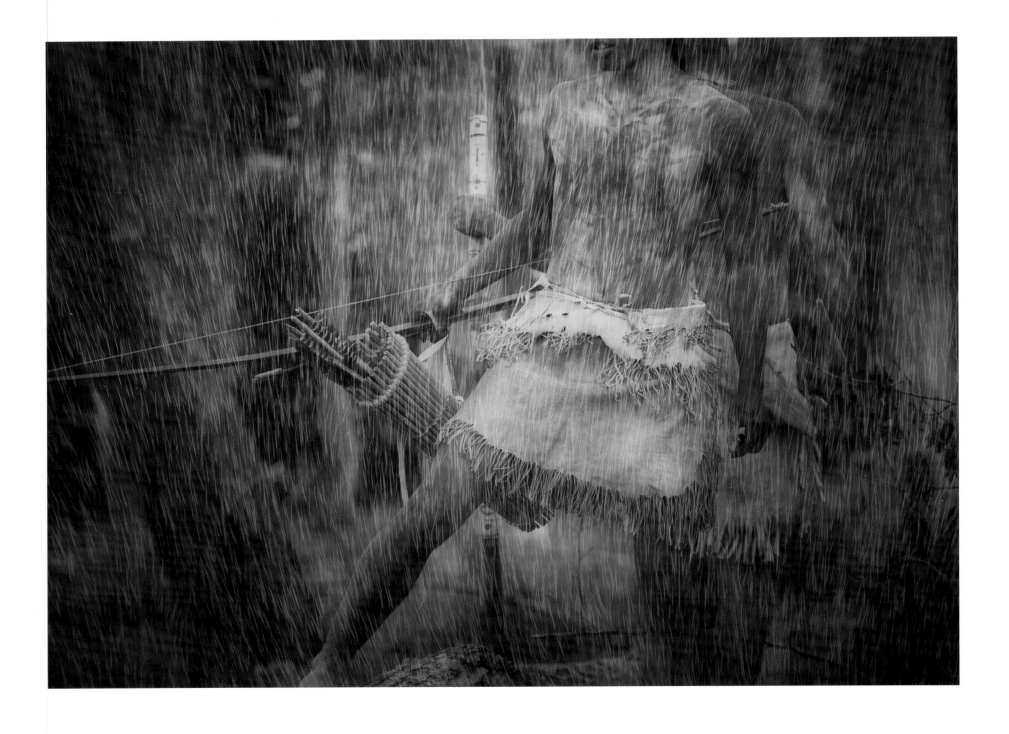

to you; but this [report] from Nansamund that you are come to destroy my Countrie, so much affrighteth all my people, as they dare not visit you; what will it availe you, to take that perforce, you may quietly have with love, or to destroy them that provide you food? What can you get by war, when we can hide our provision and flie to the woodes, whereby you must famish by wronging us your friends; and whie are you thus jealous of our loves, seeing us unarmed, and both doe, and are willing still to feed you with that you cannot get but by our labours? think you I am so simple not to knowe, it is better to eate good meate, lie well, and sleepe quietly with my women and children, laugh and be merrie with you, have copper, hatchets, or what I want, being your friend; then bee forced to flie from al, to lie cold in the woods, feed upon acorns, roots, and such trash, and be so hunted by you, that I can neither rest, eat, nor sleepe; but my tired men must watch, and if a twig but breake, everie one crie there comes Captaine Smith, then must I flie I know not whether, and thus with miserable feare end my miserable life; leaving my pleasures to such youths as you, which through your rash unadvisednesse, may quickly as miserably ende, for want of that you never knowe how to find? Let this therefore assure you of our loves and everie yeare our friendly trade shall furnish you with corne, and now also if you would come in friendly manner to see us, and not thus with your gunnes and swords, as to invade your foes.'"

In only a few lines the Chief relates where he is, where he would like to be, and where he would not like to be. His ideal of living out his life among his family and in peace is one many people would relish today, and his fear of ending his days lying cold in the woods is heartbreaking. One quiet phrase reveals the shearing effects of Smith's terrorism on the Powhatan: "if a twig but breake, everie one crie there comes Captaine Smith."

The chief describes, though in passing only, the startle response of both acute and chronic PTSD, as well as a communal fear of sudden death. The long-term effects on a people living in an unbroken fear of death and murder are still not known, though the related social morbidity of depression, anxiety, fear of the future, and suicide have all been noted in our time. More important still is another effect of such continuing fear: dissolving identity. Caught between cultures at war, a person may look for a new identity in the threatening culture, as a way to ease or seal off the effects of the trauma that comes from living in fear and depression. In addition, underlying Powhatan's words is the sad experience of having seen his people nearly die out three times in his lifetime. Few people reading this book will have seen such a loss, and it raises an essential, unanswerable question: how elastic is a society and its identity? How many times can it relax and revive before its supple bonds stretch too far and let go?

Rather than cast Powhatan in the right and Smith in the wrong, we should allow their humanity to emerge, and let them misunderstand one another on their own terms.

Smith responds to the chief's entreaty by saying,

> 'Seeing you will not rightly conceave of our words, wee strive to make you knowe our thoughts by our deeds. The vow I made you of my love, both my self and my men have kept. As for your promise I finde it everie daie violated, by some of your subjects, yet wee finding your love and kindnesse (our custome is so far from being ungratefull) that for your sake only, wee have curbed our thirsting desire of revenge, else had they knowne as wel the crueltie we use to our eneimies as our true love and curtesie to our friends. And I thinke your judgement sufficient to conceive as well by the adventures we have undertaken, as by the advantage we have by our armes of yours: that had wee intended you anie hurt, long ere this wee could have effected it: your people coming to me at James towne, are enteretained with their bowes and arrowed without exception; we esteeming it with you, as it is with us, to weare our armes as our apparell. As for the dangers of our enemies, in such warres consist of our chiefest pleasure, for your riches we have no use, as for the hiding of your provision, or by your flying to the woods, we shall so unadvisedly starve as you conclude, your friendly care in that behalfe is needlesse; for we have a rule to finde beyond your knowledge.'

Four hundred years later, I personally find Powhatan more coherent and eloquent than Smith, and the exchange even more tragic when Smith begins by admitting that the chief cannot understand what he means--and ironic since Smith wrote both speeches. We may heap abuse on Smith unadvisedly on this point, but the jumble of his words, his inability to organize thoughts and express himself, clearly seems to reveal someone hampered by post-traumatic stress. Less personally, however, his tack might simply have been to bluff and to remain as adamant as ever, for he writes that, finally, Powhatan sighed and "breathed his mind once more in this manner…." And what follows is a lament without bounds in early colonial history.

> 'Captaine Smith, I never used anie of Werowances, so kindlie as your selfe; yet from you I receave the least kindnesse of anie. Captaine Newport gave me swords, copper, cloths, a bed, tooles, or what I desired, ever taking what I offered him, and would send awaie his gunnes when I intreated him: none doth denie to laie at my feet (or do) what I desire, but onlie you, of whom I can have nothing, but what you regard not, and yet you wil have whatsoever you demand. Captain Newport you call father, and so you call me, but I see for all us both, you will doe what you list, and wee must both seeke to content you: but if you intend so friendlie as you saie, sende hence your armes that I may believe you, for you see the love I beare you, doth cause mee thus nakedlie forget my selfe.'

Although Smith does not point it out in his journal, Powhatan makes an interesting triangle in his statement: he positions himself with Captain Newport as two aggrieved men who share a common problem in the intractable Smith, who takes without giving, regardless of any downside. Powhatan sees Smith "for all us both" as a stingy and shortsighted negotiator. Smith doesn't see, as Newport does, a state in which they might all live peacefully. For a man who can only make war—not a chiefdom, as Powhatan had done—is not a chief, he is only a captain. The quiet challenge was for Smith to better himself and become a leader of the same stature shared by Newport and Powhatan. In the chief's view, then, Smith would always remain a man who could not make a deal, only a raid. Powhatan's subtle criticism undermines Smith utterly. Smith's ambitions in Virginia had brought him to his limitations in Tsenacommacoh.

Smith was relentless, however; his reputation for ferocity would compensate him nicely whether he became a leader of Powhatan's stature or not. Smith had told

Powhatan, with unwitting irony, that the English prove their beliefs with their actions, and he played the captain. Smith went on with a speech meant to keep the chief present, but gave orders for his men to break the ice in the river, and bring in the soldiers.

That winter's negotiation ended with Smith taking all the corn he wanted at gunpoint; the melting ice had allowed Smith's men to break through in a barge. Fearing for their lives, many citizens of Werowocomoco, including Powhatan, fled into the woods. We have to wonder how Smith convinced Powhatan that his life was in danger. Powhatan may have heard the stories of how the Spanish had killed other Indian leaders, and he may have thought his flight a wise move allowing him to regroup. History has shown, however, that taken in the shadow of growing terrorism, and with worse to follow, Powhatan's return to an old precedent undermined rather than bolstered the nation. The escape of so many along with their Chief would cascade through the decades into the first diaspora of Native Americans under English guns.

The Powhatan Nation had faded from enemies in the past but had survived. It probably never occurred to Powhatan that one day there would be an ultimate migration, and the loss of the ineffable parts of a nation tied to landscape. In tandem with Smith's violence, Powhatan's redeployment might have well compounded the demoralizing effects of Smith's terrorism, by sending out an increased awareness of their inability to contain the problem, applying more pressure on other tribes, and individuals, to go their own way. The new coalition might dissolve to survive.

For the moment, though, Smith had won. Warriors, "grim as divels," remained behind to guard the corn, but they assured Smith that Powhatan said they could have it. Smith took it all, with his men training their muskets on the warriors who loaded the barge. In his prose, Smith gloats over his savvy in not being tricked—by putting down his weapons, as Powhatan had asked, so that they might all be killed. The result was not the vision of friendly utopian unity that Powhatan had described for a man near the end of his

life. Smith's actions instead made it clear to Powhatan that his personal nightmare—lying cold in the woods and fleeing for his life—might well become a reality.

That afternoon Smith and his men discovered that the river was at low ebb, their barges mired in frozen muck; and so they decided until midnight to wait to sail with the tide. Throughout the dying hours of light, the Powhatan men played at sports, which Smith does not describe. While Smith and his men were laughing at how well they had done, he made plans to deal next with the Pamunkey then return and raid the capital, for hidden corn. Listening to this were two "Dutch carpenters," who were there to build Powhatan an English style house.

At nightfall, Powhatan came back into the town.

When he learned Smith was still there, he offered Smith and his men a banquet. Smith sent the two carpenters to accept the offer. They did more than accept.

They told Powhatan of Smith's intentions to raid the town. Smith and his men were relaxing and anticipating the feast when the deerskin flap drew back. The chief's "dearest jewel and daughter, in that dark night came through the irksome woods." The night air rushed in around the small figure framed against the opening. It was Pocahontas. She had grown into a young woman with long hair. She was upset. She stepped into the house, wearing deerskin, and stood amid the skins, benches, and baskets in front of the fire.

Smith stood up. He may not have seen her since the night that she and her maidens had danced for him, months earlier. He had been exploring and dealing, and had not thought of the chief's favorite daughter—except to deny accusations that he planned to marry her. But now here she was, a full presence among them.

Pocahontas spoke sparingly and directly. My father is going to

kill you. He is sending his men to feed you. They will ask you to take off your weapons. When they put the platters next to you, they will cut your throats.

The men with Smith were dumbfounded. They either had heard of or had witnessed his relationship with the girl before, and they may have heard that she had saved his life, but now it was happening in front of them. The writings of other men attest to the veracity of this scene; this rescue scene, more dangerous than the famous one, is neither dismissed nor lampooned by either Smith's contemporaries or scholars.

Smith wanted to thank Pocahontas for warning him, so he fumbled with his pouch and withdrew some beads and gave them to her. That was how he paid a guide for services and information, after all, and six beads were a lot. That should make her happy. But like many a mistaken male, he had no idea.

Pocahontas looked at the beads. She had many amber beads, but these beads of Venetian blue glass had been a sensation. They had meant something to her when she was a girl—they meant the opposite to her now. As she raised her eyes to Smith, the men saw that her face was "streaming."

If my father sees me with these, she said, he will kill me—he will know that I've been here and what I've done—and even I will not get away with it. The emotion written on her face conveyed more than her words. She had danced for him, and been rejected, and now she had risked her life for him and all he could do was thank her like a guide? That's all she was to him? She wasn't here for the glass beads. She ran "into the wild night," crying. Smith watched her go, not knowing that it would be eight years before he saw her again, and then gathered up the six beads. He would always say that she was an instrument of God in saving his life—at least on this night.

Sometime later, the flap opened and the warriors entered, bearing platters of venison, turkey and corn meal, and beans and squash and cornpone bread. The warriors suggested that the English might be more comfortable if they took off their weapons. Smith answered that, in England, it is the custom always to eat with your weapons ready. The warriors did not insist, and the meal was eaten without incident.

THE NEXT MORNING...

ALMOST DEAD FROM
GUNPOWDER BURNS ...

SMITH SAILED TO
ENGLAND.

8

I MISTAKE MYSELF

Opechancanough, the younger brother of Powhatan, met with Smith and his men, who had ventured to the capital town of the Pamunkey, following the debacle with the paramount chief. With the familiar prelude of three days of feasting and laughter behind them, Smith and Opechancanough got down to the business of trade. On the morning of the fourth day, Smith and his men walked into town and found it deserted. When Opechancanough did arrive, he was late, and he had with him a small retinue of men; others appeared at the tree line. The chief refused to deal, arguing they did not have much corn this year. Smith grew angry and said so.

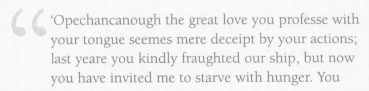

'Opechancanough the great love you professe with your tongue seemes mere deceipt by your actions; last yeare you kindly fraughted our ship, but now you have invited me to starve with hunger. You know my want, and I your plenty, of which by some meanes I must have part, remember it is fit for kings to keepe their promise. Here are my commodities, wherof take your choice; the rest I will proportion, fit bargaines for your people.'

Opechancanough accepted the deal, the details of which Smith doesn't provide, and then disappeared to take care of a few matters around town. Smith and his men walked up the lane, saw men bringing them corn and were satisfied that the deal had gone well. They retired to a house at the edge of town, where Opechancanough and his entourage would later rejoin them. As they relaxed, John Russell, one of Smith's men, following at the rear, ran up with news that they had been betrayed: 600 or 700 warriors had entered the village at the far end and were closing in. Smith was furious—but he couldn't do anything. He was caught in a trap.

Smith, in speaking to his men to bolster their spirits, blasted his superiors in London who condemned him for being so violent. "[They] will make me such a peace-breaker (in their opinions) in England, as wil break my neck; I could wish those here, that make these seeme Saints and me an oppressor." He wished this hell on the pacifists; he wanted his critics to see what happened. If his men trusted in God, they might survive, and each man swore to follow his orders—to death or freedom.

As he had been stuck in a swamp once before with Opechancanough's men, Smith was stuck again. If he and his men attacked, they might kill a few Indians, and get away alive, but the colony would starve that winter. There, in the house outside the town, Smith swung about on Opechancanough.

'I see Opechancanough your plot to murder me, but I feere it not, as yet your men and mine, have done no harme, but by our directions. Take therefore your arms; you see mine; my body shalbe as naked as yours; the Ile in your river is a fit place, if you be contented: and the conqueror (of us two) shalbe Lord and Master over all our men: otherwaies drawe all your men into the field; if you have not enough take time to fetch more, and bring what number you will, so everie one bring a basket of corne, against all which I will stake the value in copper; you see I have but 15 men, and our game shalbe conqueror take all.'

Like David and Goliath, that other trickster and giant, Smith was proposing that he and Opechancanough fight it out and let their men live. The chief was large and powerful and led a great army, but he was also in his fifties; he was not inclined to battle the stocky captain, who was half his age, much less stake his people's lives on the chance that he would win. Like Powhatan, though, Opechancanough could negotiate, and he knew that sometimes the best way to deal with Smith was to assuage his feelings—an assessment, for us, of how volatile Smith had become.

Opechancanough tried to reassure Smith that he had it all wrong—that he was overreacting: the men were just gathering as they always did, to learn what was going on. Disbelieving, Smith cautiously looked outside and saw about 300 men, thirty of whom had arrows "nocked ready to shoot."

Smith told Masters Percy and West to guard the back of the house, Powell and Beheathland to take the door. Then, in a rage, he grabbed Opechancanough by the left lock of his hair, shoved his musket barrel against the chief's chest, and "led the trembling king, (neare dead with feare) amongst all his people." Smith, who had nearly been executed by this man in the swamp, was now the man who could do the executing. He let everyone have a good look at who was in charge.

Silence filled the trees. The warriors stood stunned. Smith called out to them.

> 'I see you Pamaunkies the great desire you have to cut my throat; and my long suffering your injuries, have inboldened you to this presumption. The cause I have foreborne your insolencies, is the promise I made you (before the God I serve) to be your friend, till you give me just cause to bee your enimie….'

He continued, revealing that the time they had captured him in the swamp, almost two years earlier, drove his desire for revenge against the Powhatan at almost every encounter.

> 'I am not now at Rasseweac (halfe drownd with mire) where you tooke me prisoner, yet then for keeping your promise, and your good usage, and saving my life, I so affect you, that your denials of your treacherie, doth half perswade me to mistake my selfe….'

He was half persuaded to think, well, maybe he did have it wrong; maybe he was going crazy here. So he faltered. Almost like a Shakespearean character in mid-monologue, Smith sees himself suddenly from their view, and he might have seemed mad then, even to himself. Briefly, that is.

> 'But if I be the marke you aim at, here I stand, shoote hee that dare. You promised to fraught my ship ere I departed, and so you shall, or I meane to load her with your dead carkases; yet if as friends you wil come and trade, I once more promise not to trouble you, except you give me the first occasion.'

Smith threatened, 'We will fill the boat with corn or with your dead bodies— it's your choice.' Faced with a visibly agitated, dangerous individual, every man laid down his bow, his arrows. The Pamunkey spent the next three hours soothing Smith with adulation befitting a semi-divine personality. They heaped so much kindness and so many gifts upon him that, finally, he was worn out by the attention. He needed to rest; he went back into the longhouse to sleep. From Smith's account, it sounds as though he suffered panic exhaustion. Sometime later, Smith awoke to men entering the house; he charged up and went at them with his sword drawn. Once again, the Indian men said, Relax—we just came in to check in on you. Opechancanough apologized for the intrusion.

Smith got his hundreds of bushels of corn, but news of the way he had concluded the bargain quickly spread. Chief Powhatan was not pleased. He immediately prepared his men to exact revenge. Meanwhile, the unsuspecting Master Richard Wyffin

was making his way through the woods to Smith with news of a tragedy at the fort—several men had drowned. Wyffin happened to see Powhatan's men readying for war, but they saw him and chased him. As he ran, someone intervened and saved him. It was Pocahontas. She hid him "for a time" and pointed the warriors in the wrong direction. With her help and some bribes, Wyffin reached Smith and told him of the ambush downriver.

Smith notes, "Now so extremely Powhatan had threatened the death of his men, if they did not by some meanes kill Captaine Smith." Kill Smith or be killed. The warriors waited for Smith to appear.

Forewarned, Smith sailed downriver. Not long after they left the Pamunkey, the English came upon a field full of people offering baskets of food, provided Smith come ashore, and, as a show of friendship, do so unarmed. If the day began ominously, though, the afternoon was a series of feints, with each side leaving gifts and then withdrawing. No attack occurred. Unharmed, Smith loaded his boats with the gifts and sailed for the fort. He had made at least two more escapes. He notes in the *General History*, "Men maie think it strange there should be this stir for a little corne, but had it been gold with more ease we might have got it; and it had wanted, the whole collonie had starved." The seven-year drought scholars now think had been impinging on crops, had left the Indians with little to trade without risking starvation. When they complained of their own shortages, though, Smith, a liar, only thought they were lying.

As winter lifted into spring, and spring became summer,

Smith's tyranny and thirst for violence reached new heights.

The tribes desperately wanted peace, to find some resolution to the Smith problem—and they were willing to concede their honor to achieve that end. One day, Smith went up the James River and was attacked by Indians. Smith writes in *A General History* that once the Indians found out that it was he, Captain John Smith, with whom they were fighting, they laid down their weapons. The Indians said that they had had enough—they wanted peace. Smith claimed credit for the peace, boasting that his awe-inspiring stature prompted submission everywhere he went—because he was insuperable. The Indians didn't see it this way; for them, acquiescence was the only way to placate and survive this volatile and terrifying individual, a terrorist who held them hostage, and burned houses and canoes and crops, seasons of their work, if they ever failed to please him.

When the Indians asked for peace, Smith writes, "Their Orator was a lustie young fellow called Okanindge, whose worthy discourse deserveth to be remembred."

"'Captaine Smith, my Master is here present in the company, thinking it Captaine Winne, and not you, (of him he intended to have beene revenged) having never offended him. If he hath offended you in escaping your imprisonment, the fishes swim, the foules fly, and the very beasts strive to escape the snare and live. Then blame not him being a man. He would intreat you remember, you being a prisoner, what paines he tooke to save your life. If since he had injured you he was compelled to it: but howsoever, you have revenged it with our too great losse. We perceive and well know you intend to destroy us, that are here to intreat and desire your friendship, and to enjoy our houses and plant our fields, of whose fruit you shall participate: otherwise you will have the worse by our absence; for we can plant any where, though with more labour, and we know you cannot live if you want our harvest, and that reliefe we bring you. If you promise us peace, we will believe you; if you proceed in revenge we will abandon the Country.'"

Okanindge's appeal is stunning. It speaks of how much the English relied on the Indians to survive. Its assertion of Smith's barbarity—"our too great losse"—is a morbid validation of Smith's method. The threat to leave, however, is tragic. The Indians' leaving did not have the desired result: the English did starve en masse, but the Indians' absence only whetted in the English a desire to possess the abandoned land.

On a quieter note, it is interesting to think that the chief of whom Okanindge speaks, Wowinchopunk of the Paspahegh, had once been a friend of Smith's. He had intervened with Powhatan to save Smith's life while he was held captive—a story never mentioned by Smith. For reasons Smith does not detail lucidly—yet which entail his pursuit of the carpenters who had returned to steal weapons for Powhatan—the two men fought a hand-to-hand battle arising from that chase, and the chief became Smith's prisoner. Smith refused to release the chief, despite the pleas of his family. The chief finally escaped. (Various engravings of 1624 depict a tiny Smith holding the giant captive at sword or musket point, variously either Wowinchopunk or Opechancanough; a modern interpretation suggests the image symbolizes the little island and the New World it would soon hold hostage.)

As summer wore on, the combination of Smith's power as the colony's president and his reputation for bloodlust among the Indians had put him into an untenable position. The colonials were beginning to regard Smith as a liability, despite the successes of his explorations, contributions, and negotiations. In their growing opinion, Smith's volatility would provoke the Powhatan into killing the colonials in retaliation. The fear was not unfounded; if anything, the men back in the fort had every reason to worry. Those around Smith saw him as a man increasingly out of control, whereas he saw himself as a man increasingly in control. Smith lost allies—even George Percy, a friend and untainted writer of the colony's history, turned on Smith, describing him as "ambitious, unworthy, and vainglorious," a man

insatiable for power, who would destroy the colony's principles to become its supreme leader. Smith drove the men into aligning themselves in spirit with the Indians of the Powhatan nation.

By late summer 1609, Chief Powhatan was furious with his newly adopted son, who had let him down repeatedly with broken promises. On their first meeting, at the end of 1607, Smith had told him that the English were taking refuge from the Spanish ships, that they would be leaving soon. Now they had houses and a church, and every so often a ship came with more people—and just recently a fleet of seven ships had brought 300 people. Smith had not traded with weapons, either, nullifying Powhatan's plan to gain power over the surrounding nations. Still worse, Smith had promised that the English would stay on the island, but Powhatan had seen people move upriver and start farms, well inside his nation, a clear violation of the deal. Powhatan could tolerate the English if they were a boon to him with copper and weapons, but if they were only trespassing and manipulating him, then they had to go.

Ironically, the ships that had arrived that summer—after eluding the hurricane that sank one ship and grounded the *Sea Venture* on the shoals of Bermuda—carried men who agreed with Powhatan that Smith was a problem. The three captains in charge of the ships were the three men that Smith had demanded the Virginia Company not send back: Captains Gabriel Archer, John Ratcliffe, and John Martin not only despised Smith, they wanted him gone. They were not alone. With them were a number of men known as the "unruly gallants," convicted men of a dicey and debauched mentality who had chosen life in the colony over time in prison. If Smith had resented the lazy gentlemen of the colony's first consignment of men, he really hated the criminals.

The mood at the fort was contentious after the arrival of the seven ships. All of Smith's innovations came undone; the new arrivals saw no reason to conform to Smith's demands, and many of the men who had been there for a while had grown sick of his despotic ways: anyone who rebelled got a whipping or a beating. The men loathed him enough to want him dead. Rumors were wild: Smith was trying to make himself the king of Virginia and subjugate his enemies in the fort; he wanted to marry Pocahontas, dominate the New World, and leave behind England. He was cutting deals with tribes outside the Powhatan nation. To top it all off, he wore buckskin, which outraged some of the colonials, who thought he had lost his mind.

The old rumors about him and the chief's daughter gained new believers among the unruly gallants. Smith denied the accusation hotly. Writing many years later, he stresses one thing— that had he wanted to marry her, no one could have stopped him. But he had *not* tried to marry her or become king of Virginia. Nevertheless, his enemies continued to slander him. He had lied so often to the Indians that the English concluded that he was lying to them, too. Smith insisted that he only lied to the Indians, but the Trickster was only tricking himself.

The men voted him out as president, stripping him of his power over them. Recognizing his value as a negotiator, they sent him out to trade for corn. It is a move that could be open to interpretation. The men knew that the Indians were very near to reaching a breaking point with regard to Smith. It would not be too great a supposition to think that the English sent him out to trade with the desire that the Indians would dispense of Smith for them.

Smith had escaped killing at the hands of the Indians several times by the end of summer, going back to Powhatan's and Opechancanough's attempts in January. The third incident, Smith alleges, had occurred during a break in the trade negotiations, when the Indians brought his men poisoned drink. Smith was going to die, however, if the English had any say in the matter. The colonials were sick of him nearly getting them killed with his cruelty and treachery toward the Indians; they were sick of his arrogance, his attempts to make himself king. When fighting broke out between colonials and warriors in a nearby village upriver, Smith was sent to make peace. In this intricate dance of loyalty and betrayal, Smith had sent men up the river as a protective force, part of a trade agreement with the Powhatan, but they were out of control. They beat and robbed the Indians, who complained to Smith that his men were even worse than the Monacans—and the Indians told him that they would have to seek reprisal. Smith could not reason with his own men and sailed down the river. Although only twelve Indians seem to have attacked that day, they killed many men and created mass panic among the one hundred English. Downriver, the Powhatan agreed to peace, but upriver the wounded claimed to their Captain West that Smith had orchestrated the turmoil in a power move to become king.

In the months to come, to justify what happened next, many of the colonials who hated Smith—had suffered his whippings and beatings— all vowed that Smith had conspired with the Powhatan to kill Captain West and his hundred men—an accusation Smith hotly denied; with only five men, he could not have engaged the fight and lived. And yet, not all captains die in the field; some are killed by their own men.

Smith almost didn't get back to Jamestown. One afternoon, as he took a nap on deck, someone put a fuse to the bag of powder that

rode on his belt. The powder exploded—possibly set off by the fuse of his own matchlock musket, which was always lit. Percy wrote that it "shrewdly" blew up, curiously assigning intelligence to the freak accident. The blast blew off muscle and flesh in a ten-inch square hole, and with his clothes on fire, Smith hurled himself into the river, where he nearly drowned. In agony, he managed to pull himself on board. He was almost out of his mind with pain, and when they finally got him to bed, seventy-five miles later in Jamestown, it was his own visible agony that saved him.

Sometime that night, he awoke. Standing there against the flicker of the low fire were two silhouettes, with muskets aimed at his head. It was two men loyal to West. Coe and Dyer's mission was to kill him, Smith wrote. But in light of his injuries, and his senselessness with pain, they took pity on him. The next morning, October 1st of 1609, almost dead from third-degree burns and what he called the "pitiable" loss of his flesh, Smith sailed to London. In the *General History*, he named names, and defended himself, explaining that he had left the colony with so much meat, corn, and other food they should have survived the winter.

Later that year, while recovering, Smith had occasion to read a popular Spanish account of colonizing that appeared in print under the name *Virginia Richly Valued*. The story features a remarkable scene: Juan Ortiz, captured in Florida, is about to be burned at the stake when the daughter of Chief Ucita suddenly intervenes and saves his life. Whether this account sparked for Smith a memory or an idea for a new story of his own, we will never know.

A young Indian woman visited Jamestown one afternoon in late fall. The colonials stared at the famous Pocahontas. Her hair was long; she wore a leather skirt. She inquired after Smith, perhaps having heard of his wounds. The new people at the fort, rough people all, treated her badly. He's dead, they told her. They may have lied to wound her, or his death may have seemed inevitable to them—regardless, they made it clear that she was not welcome at the fort anymore.

Pocahontas assessed them, the deplorable fort behind them, and may have found them contemptible. Her sympathy had been always with Smith rather than the English. When she walked away that afternoon, she turned her back on them for what she must have imagined would be the rest of her life, and returned to the communal world she knew.

The English watched her walk toward the trees. They may have felt all was right again. Order, English order, had been restored. Smith had been expelled and the savages snubbed. They locked the gates and any possibility to learn. Yet in snubbing the paramount chief's daughter, they also may have closed off any chance for aid from Powhatan. That winter almost every one of them would starve with their haughty incompetence and regrets intact.

Pocahontas may have been sick over the news of Smith's death, and given accounts of how freely Indian women expressed their emotions, it would not be surprising if she strayed off that afternoon and wept—for him and for the compound grief and difficulty of her time and situation. She was a young woman of her society, but the impression Smith had made on her while she matured was clearly profound.

Not long after she returned to her father with the news of Smith's death, a runner came to the fort with a gift—it was Smith's compass. If anyone at the fort read the symbolism of Powhatan returning the compass, no one wrote it down.

AFTER THE ENGLISH

KIDNAPPED HER,

POCAHONTAS

WAS ISOLATED

BUT NEVER

ALONE.

Powhatan invited the English to visit and trade for corn.

Captain Ratcliffe and a contingent of thirty men sailed up the York River. No record of the event has survived, revealing how well or poorly the feasting and negotiating went—but the killing was complete. Ratcliffe was captured and tortured to death by the women, and his men died in an ambush. Only a young boy named Henry Spelman escaped. He was saved by Pocahontas.

She absconded north with him and gave him into the care of the Patawomek, with whom he spent the next year. She, too, decided to remain. Why she stayed is unclear; we only know that the last time she crossed her father, by warning Smith, she said that her father would kill her were he to find out. He might never have known that she had warned Smith, or, her saving Spelman may have forced her to save herself. She may have come to a crisis that was so unusual among her people that she could only resolve the tension by improvising in a traditional way—by moving on and starting anew inside the coalition.

We may believe this story, that he was captured and taken north, if we believe Smith's tale of how Spelman came to live among the Indians.

Henry Spelman tells a different story, though, and his version reminds

us of all the ways in which fact and fantasy intertwine. In the mode of high adventure, he briskly and vividly takes us down his own labyrinth of misunderstanding, friendship, and killing. He says simply that Smith sold him to Pocahontas's brother, Parahunt, the werowance of a tribe on the James and a man whom the English called Little Powhatan. Spelman lived with him and learned the language, in the tradition of exchanging hostages to ensure peace and translate with finesse the nuances of language and culture. At some point the chief of the Patawomek came to visit and was so friendly toward Henry, Thomas Savage, and a youth known as Samuel, that the three youths decided to go and live with that chief, instead. Some distance down the path, Savage demurred and went back, but the others carried on, even after Parahunt sent men to find them and get them back. While they were hiking through the woods north to his new home, one of the Patawomek men inexplicably killed Samuel with a hatchet to the head—perhaps he was young man saved by Pocahontas, and who Smith incorrectly identified as Spelman. Spelman fled into the woods, eventually making his way to the Patawomek capital, where the overtly friendly chief took him in.

Henry might tell the truth, and his tales charmed the English on his return to the colony, but a cautionary note needs to be sounded: some of his contemporaries thought him a malicious liar, and he does get some things wrong—like child sacrifice, which Rolfe disproved later. Regardless, Spelman creates a detailed, rude, and lively picture of Indian life that flickers like a black-and-white film. With even less polish than Smith's, Spelman's account makes the better writers like William Strachey, George Percy, and Ralph Hamor seem distant, in spite of their superior style and understanding—or perhaps for that reason. His account is not a sentimental affair with the Noble Savage, and its images of how tough the women were and how rough life was for them give us an idea of the difficulties that Pocahontas might have endured in marriage, if she spoke out.

One day when the chief went to visit another tribe, he left Henry behind with his wives. One of them ordered Henry to carry one of her children on a daylong journey of her own. He refused, and in exasperation, she hit him three or four times. When it seemed that she was going to strike him again, he grabbed her hair, pulled her down, and began punching her. Several other wives jumped in and beat him so badly that he thought he was lamed. When the chief came home, Spelman told him what had happened. The chief took a paring iron and struck one wife in the head. She fell to the floor, apparently dead. Spelman, scared that the chief would next turn on him, fled to a neighbor's house. Spelman had witnessed many punishments by then—a thief had his brains knocked out; a murderer was beaten until all his bones were broken and then, while still alive, was thrown into a fire. The next morning, the chief found him and told him not to worry, he loved him, and would care for him—and his wife, who was back on her feet, scowled malevolently at Henry.

In light of this story and others, the condition of Pocahontas's life becomes apparent. This act of hers, to rescue a boy and then to run away from her father, hints at an ulterior conflict she may have lived with under her father's domination. Her pattern of intervening against her father's wishes, rescuing his enemies—Richard Wyffin, Smith and his fifteen men, to name just a couple of occasions—seems to reiterate an even deeper desire to rescue herself from her father. Naturally, the idea is speculative, but, given what is known of Pocahontas, one can consider that her actions reveal the torque she felt between two cultures and her own maturing sense of autonomy. For a woman who made her own decisions, her self-discovery may have chafed the men around her, as it did her father—and, possibly, any man who courted her.

Assuming that she was obsessed with Smith—and there is evidence in London, eight years later, that she was—then the news of his death would have been heart-wrenching for her. She would say

in London that she never knew for sure that he had died because the English "will lie much." Most telling is not the uncertainty, but that she held onto it for eight years—not just in grief but in hope.

Although our ideas of bereavement will never reveal those of the Powhatan, scientists believe that brain chemistry is panhuman. Grief for a loved one is a compound loss. If Pocahontas's thoughts for Smith had followed an arc of infatuation, then she would have experienced something tantamount to a withdrawal from powerful drugs, for research shows that a person's levels of dopamine and serotonin drop following the end of a love, inducing a state of despondency. Believing Smith was dead, she likely went through her days in abstraction, present without being present. With the chemistry of infatuation and obsession in play, she may have lived on a natural high that she had never felt before she knew him, one that had been imprinted to such a degree that she could only feel happy and normal if she were able to reproduce that sensation with another man. Any man who failed to help her regain that high would have left her feeling bereft or incomplete. The loss of the loved one would have been masked as a growing estrangement.

After Pocahontas learned of Smith's alleged death,

Kecoum, a young captain among the Patawomek warriors, began courting her and eventually won her favor—a year, perhaps, into her mourning. He most likely purchased her from Powhatan in a traditional marriage ritual. Spelman records that the marriage of two people required the groom to purchase the bride. The couple broke a string of beads over their clasped hands, then gave the beads as payment to the bride's father, who brought her to the ceremony; "much mirth and feasting" followed. The marriage did not last. They divorced the Indian way, with a marvelous economy of words: each only had to say "I divorce you" three times. Kecoum is the only Indian husband of hers whose name survives, but she may have married and divorced another as well—whether she could not connect with the men, who offered her a traditional way of life, or could not get over her loss of Smith, is not known.

If we follow an alternate story path, rather than the one in which she absconds with Henry, Pocahontas lived among her people and was divorced when she came into the Patawomek country in the winter of 1613. She was representing her father in negotiations with various people from the Potomac River region and north, who had come to the Patawomek capital to broker trades. The negotiations stretched to three months. She was a guest of the Patawomek chief, but she was also said to be "living alone, unknown to all but a few trusty friends." Her own developing sense of autonomy may have led her to separate herself and perhaps pursue living on her own somewhere else, where she might begin again. She had gone against her father more than once, and feared that her father had reason to kill her for at least one of her transgressions. By living in seclusion, she might have felt safer.

But just as Smith did not see the wide circle closing in around him, she did not see it, either—and its loose array was put in place by a privateer named Samuel Argall, who also came to the Patawomek capital during the trade negotiations of 1613, sent by the Jamestown colonists. The colonists had experienced difficult times in the years following Smith's departure.

In the fall of 1609, the demise of Ratcliffe and his men did not unduly alarm the colonists; however, when other expeditions sallied forth to negotiate for corn, they died fighting as well. The two carpenters returned to Powhatan again, but annoyed with their treachery, he had their brains bashed out. Whether Smith's behavior had prompted the reprisals is unknown, but the English soon wished they had not gotten rid of Smith—it seemed he alone could prevail in negotiations with the Indians. By wintertime, the colonists had depleted the stores of corn that Smith had managed to acquire in September. The locals had stolen or killed the hundreds of hogs they had left on Hog Island just a few miles downstream

because the colonials were afraid to leave the fort. Every time someone left the fort to forage or to answer nature's call, the Indians killed that person. The fort soon became an empty warehouse, open to arrows from above, and an open latrine.

The colonists ate anything they could find

within the confines of the fort. They grabbed mice and dug snakes out of the ground. They ate rats, oysters, and fish, and finally the sheep, cows, horses, and horsehides. Trusting dogs and supple cats went into the pot. Boiling their shirts gave them edible starch. By midwinter, many people were dying, buried quickly at night. The situation grew more desperate: they ate leather belts and shoes and book covers; even the leather door hinges were boiled. When they ran out of animals, a few turned to humans. An Indian killed and buried near the fort was dug up and eaten. One man staggered about raving at the sky why God had forsaken them; he was killed shortly thereafter by Indian arrows. Some dug their own graves, laid in them, and waited to die. One man, in the throes of his hunger, killed his wife and ate her. Men hanged him by his thumbs until he confessed and then executed him—it seems no one ate him, though the morbid joke went round about the recipe for grilled wife. The winter of 1609–1610 came to be known as the Starving Time. Of the 500 or 600 people who had waved goodbye to Smith in the fall of 1609, only about sixty were still alive come May of 1610, when two small ships pulled up to the island. They carried the passengers of the *Sea Venture*, the ship presumed lost the previous summer in a hurricane.

John Rolfe brimmed his eyes and gazed at the near and distant figures dotting the sand and wading in the surf. He gave thanks to his Lord for saving him a few hours earlier, when a hurricane had overtaken the *Sea Venture*, one of a fleet of ships that had set out from England in early 1608 carrying new colonists to Virginia.

The other ships had last been seen in mid-tempest, blown high over the crest and then seemingly into oblivion on the other side. In the close quarters of the *Sea Venture*, 150 men and women were thrown about with all matter of objects and animals as the ship pitched and yawed and then rolled—a combination of motions that caused the passengers to convulse violently. The hold filled with water; there wasn't a leak, the caulking had been stripped. After three days of sickening upheaval, the captain decided a carefully aimed crash-landing on Bermuda offered the best chance of survival.

As Rolfe stood on wet sand in the windy July sunshine, with wreckage in the distance, his piety was not a façade. In spite of overwhelming grief—his daughter, Bermuda, was born and later died on the island, and his wife would die shortly after they reached Virginia—and trying ordeals, he seems to have been a man who saw the miraculous hand of his Lord in the most exasperating nightmares. One such miracle happened to him while he wandered about the island's interior. He came across a local variety of a plant that he recognized; it looked robust and interesting. He pulled it by the root; it was tobacco.

The survivors on Bermuda salvaged pieces of the *Sea Venture*

and for nine months worked to build two small ships, the *Deliverance* and the *Patience*—named with that familiar if unwitting irony. Even though they could leave now, more than a few of the survivors wanted to remain on the island rather than return to the rigid structure of English life—the same call that Smith had heard so clearly. But they all set sail, and by May of 1610 they were navigating up the James River, almost a year late, to their new home and refuge, Jamestown.

They had no idea that the Starving Time had decimated the colony. There is no telling what revulsion and pity played in their faces when they came ashore at last, only to find an open latrine,

tumbledown walls, houses burned for wood, and a few dozen wretches in rags, gaunt of face and frame, shuffling out to meet them. May in Virginia can rise hot and stifling, the sky white with haze, clothes sticking to skin. Rolfe must have looked about and wondered what his Lord had in mind for him this time— the pile of fecal matter, the muddy field of the dead, and the collapse of houses and spirit were beyond anything he had seen. They were fortunate, indeed, though, for as they learned, almost everyone in their original fleet, who had escaped the hurricane the previous summer, had died of starvation. The unruly gallants were gone. In a summary vote, the decision was clear: everyone decided to give up. The transplant of English life would not take; the body geographic had rejected the foreign graft.

Against communal lethargy and despair, it took some time to break down the colony. In early June, everyone in Jamestown—survivors and newcomers alike—boarded the *Deliverance* and the *Patience*. Behind them the fort stood intact; none of the English had had the energy to burn the place they despised, so they left it to rot and fall down. They sailed to the mouth of the James, where they sank anchor. In the morning, they would sail for London.

At dawn, however, an enormous sail breached the horizon and tacked toward them. It was the massive warship *De La Warr*, with Lord De La Warr himself on board; more ships followed in its wake, carrying more settlers and enough provisions to last a year. (De La Warr would make himself infamous in the colony. Most heinous of all, perhaps, was the day he had Indian women and

children thrown overboard and shot in the head as they foundered next to the ship. It was a bit of revenge for their tribe having killed Ratcliffe's party of men the previous fall.) De La Warr gave the order for the starvelings and survivors to turn around and sail back to James Fort, one of the various grand names given to the muddy sump. The English experiment that had died of natural causes overnight had that morning an artificial heart and a pulse.

Improvements began right away, with rebuilding and planting, and in the next few years Jamestown righted itself, though with faltering success, for the plantation still could not produce any one commodity that would make a profit for its investors. More stock had been sold to continue financing the venture, but in London the partners and investors were impatient to recoup their losses and to quit themselves of this idea, permanently.

Thomas Gates, one of the Bermuda castaways, was put in charge of the colony. If the colonists felt that they had suffered enough already, Gates was there to show them what suffering really was; and though he was replaced a year later by Sir Thomas Dale, both men led a tyranny against the colonials, one so heinous that many of them risked their lives to switch sides and live with the Indians. Both tyrants were sadists who robed themselves in piety and military discipline to justify and then to relish their cruelties. Gates instituted martial law; he outlined the series of rules and codes of conduct in a book he called *The Laws Divine, Moral and Martial*. Any infringement of the laws would result in severe punishment. When Dale arrived and took over leadership of the colony in May 1611, he kept the laws in place; the people of Jamestown suffered them until 1618, when they were repealed.

The laws present us with a reverse-image, or negative, of life inside the colony. Capital crimes that carried the death penalty included stealing vegetables; killing livestock without permission; denouncing the colony or a colonist; missing church three times; mocking the Bible or Christianity; failing to swear an oath of allegiance to the Anglican church; taking a ship belonging to the colony without permission; trading with the Indians without permission; or speaking in a way that might be construed as sedition against the church, colony, or its leaders. Oddly, considering the English attitude toward the Indians, the death penalty was also imposed for the crime of robbing an Indian who had come to the fort to trade. In spite of their hostility and theft of land, the English still imagined themselves as tolerant purveyors of Christianity.

Lesser offenses earned sentences that were more than harsh. Two women who sewed two shirts a tad short were hauled out, stripped, tied to stakes, and publicly whipped. Swearing might get the offender a bobbin through the tongue for the second offense—and death the third time. As severe as this seems, though, the laws were in synch with their time, an era when the Spanish Inquisition was torturing people, the better to receive their Catholic rewards.

Although the brutality began with Gates, Dale quickly outshone him for sheer barbarity. To be fair, like other abusers, Dale felt provoked. Upon his arrival, he found the fort's lanes filled with wastrels who spent their days "bowling in the streets" against a backdrop of small plots of corn and thatch-roofed cottages slapped together with clay and wooden walls. In Dale's eyes, the colonials deserved to be punished, and the punishment would improve their souls. While some societies rely on the external discipline of the tyrant to carry on, others rely on the internal self-discipline of the citizen for order. Smith had tried to impose the latter, but failed, so Dale would impose the former with terror.

The Natural approach, endorsed by Smith, was now placed against an authoritarian approach of Anglo-Christendom, and the results gave the Indians a reason to rethink their dealings with the English. Far south, in the bloody chaparral of the Spanish Empire, native people had already pointed out the hypocrisy of murdering people to save them. The Powhatan and other peoples in the English colonies had the same problem with euro-hypocrisy, though the English did not convert by the sword. These religious themes point us toward a difference in concrete and metaphorical thinking, a sphere for misunderstanding between the cultures.

The Powhatan and other native peoples were concrete thinkers: love meant love; promise meant promise. To them, the idea that someone might use love to kill, or use a promise to lie was unheard of and alien. The Naturals, therefore, meant what they said and said what they meant, while the English were able to mean what they said, contingent upon changing their mind later, or mean something in a metaphoric or symbolic way only, and not literally at all. The Powhatan were certainly able to confuse an opponent with dinner and trade, but gestures of friendliness were not sworn agreements. The Powhatan found that English actions and words always varied, and unpredictably so—to the Indians' disadvantage. Such an essential duplicity throws another light onto the laws divine, moral and martial. In short, the deeper hypocrisy is that the English would treat the English far worse than the Indians did, when they had to deal with themselves. By modern standards, the Indians were more than liberal; they were tragically lenient. And they felt revulsion for the Christians who killed their own for the high motivation of spiritual love.

The remorseless Dale was adept at administering pain and punishment and inept at providing food. Imagine how bad life must have been for some colonists to run off to the Indians, people

who might kill them. Even worse for the runaway, the Indians might return him to the fort. Dale was a man of Inquisitional nastiness, and he inflicted torture and death on the returned runaways: He shot them, hanged them, burned them, tied them to trees and let them starve, and tortured them on the wheel and rack. He showed them no mercy, ironically a Christian virtue that he preached about to the Indians. Other punished colonials hobbled about in leg chains for years and described themselves as "slaves" in a penal colony.

As for the Indians, Dale suited a hundred men in armor, and without provocation sent them south of the James against the Nansemond—who, upon seeing their arrows ricochet off the men, prayed to Okeus for rain to put out the matchlock muskets. Okeus did not answer their prayers. The Indians began to concede that Okeus had not favored them with weapons as the English God had favored the English. Although a minor moment in the chaos, this one about gods indicates that the Indians were now on a psychological down-slope, below the English. (They even came to a point when they wanted to deal with Smith again. What Smith threatened, the new leaders did.)

The assumption that one's inferiority stems from a want of technology eventually would seep into and poison the native and enslaved peoples of America—for only the superior, so the thinking goes, could make this world's complex structures, visible and invisible alike. In the Indian's lamentable observation that Okeus had not favored them with guns, one can hear the very first sounding of an inference that would grow over time into the overt racism and purported superiority of others. It would infect minorities with a

concept of insufficiency that would help defeat them for centuries to follow. While such a conclusion, that one god is more powerful than another, might seem obvious to anyone in those straits, that demoralizing idea is a construct for those who accept themselves in their god-given world. People who invent themselves, like Smith, are accused of arrogance or sedition, which is aimed at undermining such confidence. For Pocahontas, whose confidence often seems adamant, any notion of inferiority was likely unthinkable.

Throughout this time, Smith, in London, continued to lambaste the Virginia Company in letters for its stupidity in not letting the colony grow its own food, for not appointing the right men for the right job, for not paying Indians for their land rather than taking it, and thereby secure a continuing peace—one of his remarkable, late innovations.

The company's executives didn't care to listen to the man who had been condemned as an arrogant self-promoter. They left all improvements to the imagination of Dale. He overruled all of Smith's innovations that had stemmed in large part from the Naturals and installed ideas that grew straight out of the feudal era. Under the flag of the Virginia Company, Dale transformed the plantation of Jamestown into a death camp—a forerunner of the great southern plantations that would soon grace the state. Dale's actions seeded the Middle Ages into the start of America, with incalculable iniquity and tragedy.

Two divergent kinds of ambition were driving Jamestown. The one for individuals, which Smith had embodied, would create small tobacco farmers. The feudal one developed by Dale would morph into tobacco plantations. The former would become the analog of the American whom we continue to raise up as a sentimental standard—the small farmer. The latter would be a sentimental emulation of European grandeur, one so inherently false that it would transmogrify into the Civil War. Under various banners of states rights and taxes and slavery, the founding tensions between the individual and the corporation that beset Jamestown would clash some two and a half centuries later to the near apocalyptic destruction of Virginia and the South.

One of Dale's biggest achievements was the building of a settlement on an upriver bend of the James in autumn 1611. Built by 350 men under incoming arrows, Henricus—later Henrico, named for Prince Henry, son of King James—became a real working village, and something of a crucial symbol to those in London who were anxious for the colony to survive. With some 700 colonials split between Jamestown and Henrico, England had taken a long step into the interior; the New World would be English in time and nature.

Nevertheless, Powhatan had not gone away, and his raids continued to kill colonists and add to the colony's sagging morale. In 1611, knowing that it was pointless to try to trade with Powhatan, Dale turned to privateer Samuel Argall, who had recently burned down a French settlement in the New York area, and asked him to find corn for the approaching winter. Argall knew where to look: he had enjoyed success before with the Patawomek, who were not fond of Powhatan. His trip was a success in more ways than one: he acquired 1,100 pounds of corn; he purchased the freedom of the ecstatic Henry Spelman, who soon sailed for London; and

most important, he learned strategic information.

Argall discovered that Pocahontas, the famous daughter of Powhatan, lived among the Patawomek. Her years—or months, depending on accounts—with them, had not gone well. The women did not like her haughty behavior and were rude to her. She lived in the woods alone, and had divorced Kecoum. She was also seeking to live in obscurity. The playful, high-spirited girl whom the English had known had turned into a reclusive young woman content, it would seem, to live her life alone and on her terms. This antisocial turn seems to speak of a continuing sadness and estrangement from the people she knew, as if she had embraced her various losses and grown a new persona around them. For myriad reasons, then, only a few friends knew who she was and where—but no one else.

No one argues over what happened next, though for sheer romance this next episode in her life is every bit as grand as the legend that she saved John Smith. In the spring of 1613, Argall returned to the Patawomek to trade for corn and to capture Pocahontas with cunning; he knew he could not take her by force. His reasons were apparent to Dale and the other colonists: if he could take her hostage, she could be used to leverage Powhatan into stopping his war of attrition against them and returning seven English captives and the guns and swords he had obtained through various means. Argall met with a friend of his, Japazaws, the brother to the chief of the Patawomek, and laid out his plans.

Japazaws didn't like the plan, and his brother liked it even less. The chief of the Patawomek said that taking Powhatan's daughter would start a war. Argall assured the chief that the English would protect the Patawomek from the Powhatan, and further, that failing to help take Pocahontas hostage would ruin their personal friendship, as men and brothers. The decision to help the English took a few days. The Patawomek were unhappy with the reasoning, but the real politics surrounding Powhatan had come into play. As scholars point out, sitting on the Potomac River, the Patawomek were at the far northern edge of the coalition and enjoyed little protection from Powhatan, and much worse, the ever elusive tipping point had resurfaced. The Patawomek saw the future, and it was full of Englishmen, not Powhatans. They sided with the English.

Japazaws enlisted his wife to help in a charade to capture Pocahontas. They found Pocahontas and got her down to the landing site, where Argall's ship stood at anchor. When Argall invited them on board, nothing would do until they all went on. Japazaws told his wife, No—you are a woman; you need a female escort. The wife threw a pluperfect fit that she couldn't go onboard. He finally threatened to beat her if she didn't subside. So, they asked Pocahontas, Could she help? She would only have to go onboard.

Pocahontas refused all entreaties. No doubt she had heard well enough by then what became of those who went on board ships: they got thrown overboard and shot in the head, or were kidnapped. An odd note about this moment is that she was alone— no one attended to her as befitting the paramount chief's daughter.

Tired of the whining, Pocahontas finally agreed. They went on board and walked about. After lunch, Argall led her to the gunner's quarters for a nap, but she soon came out, anxious to leave. Argall blocked her way. He told her that she was now his prisoner, and that he would use her to negotiate for peace with her father. Japazaws and his wife threw their hands in the air and feigned outrage. Their part in the plot was revealed, however, when Argall gave them a copper kettle in thanks for the deception. They left immediately.

Pocahontas was shocked. Japazaws was a werowance of a nearby tribe and his wife was her friend, but both had just sold her out for a kettle. They could not have done this deed without the foreknowledge of the Patawomek head chief. That she knew those involved in her kidnapping confounded her. Smith may have been the only man until then ever consistent with her; she always knew where she stood with him—on the other side of No. Her lessons may have been falling along a theme now— how betrayal, and little else, may come from those whom we trust.

When he learned of her kidnapping, Smith wrote furiously against it, regardless of its ostensible mission. He was outraged at Argall for deceiving her and at the Patawomek for abetting Argall; he wrote as a man who knew very closely how that betrayal would hurt her, and who knew what she had done for him and the others who would have died without her. He wrote of her weeping and begging to be released; Ralph Hamor, the colony's historian, described her as "despondent and pensive." Smith may have dramatized and Hamor may have it right. This is not a matter of presentation; her resiliency is what matters here and the degree to which she would prove malleable to everything that soon followed.

Curiously, and perhaps because she was famous, she was not treated as a prisoner, but rather as a celebrity—a new path that her life would follow to its end. In Jamestown, she was received and treated well, for she was more than a prisoner to them—a figure of the future, if possible. They imagined that her father would deal quickly for her release; instead, he amazed them all by not trading at all. After asking them to treat Pocahontas well, Powhatan sent a canoe full of corn and the men they asked for, but not the swords or the guns. As he once had hesitated to kill the English, he now hesitated to negotiate for Pocahontas's return, though he was said to be grievously sad.

The English were astonished by his reluctance to deal for his daughter's freedom; Pocahontas may not have been. After all, she had crossed him by saving Smith and his men, may have by saving Spelman-- or Samuel--and possibly by divorcing Kecoum. If she felt the strain of loving a father who might kill her, Powhatan might have felt the strain of loving a daughter who continually betrayed him. She seems to have sent no personal words to her father once captured. Her silence indicates a falling out that must have been disheartening for them both. Her attempt to live in seclusion and anonymity among the

Patawomek, however briefly, outlines a young woman who would rather give up and remain where she is, against her possible fears of rape and execution by the English. She had seen other hostages taken and returned; it was the normal way of life then.

The English moved her upriver to better-defended Henricus. The settlement stood on what was then the shifting southern perimeter of Powhatan's nation, which had slid north to avoid the invasion. After the English kidnapped her, Pocahontas was isolated but never alone. Her female attendants were ordered to treat her gently, so she would not have anything to complain of when returned to her father. When the colonists had lied to her a few years earlier, telling her that Smith was dead, she had known grief and had withdrawn from life. Now, in the autumnal hush of the fields around Henricus, Pocahontas began to find new life, recovering and discovering herself in the kindly hands, gestures, and faces of her enemies, lulled and entranced by their attention. Although she may not have feared for her life, she was sliding, in effect, into an early transformative phase of feeling affection for her captors. The immersion in Christian love was more than intense: it was seductive, and the seducer had a nice face.

THE MARRIAGE

WAS COMPLETE AND WITH IT CAME EIGHT YEARS OF PEACE,

AS POWHATAN SWORE TO BRING AN END

TO ANY AND ALL HOSTILITY AGAINST

THE COLONIALS.

She first saw him in church,

where she was taken frequently. As she rose to leave one day, she met the eye of a bearded young man who was about twenty-eight years old, and in appearance not unlike her dead friend. John Rolfe was smooth where John Smith had been rough. As she watched him over the next few months, she saw more that was unfamiliar in him than she had seen in Smith or had known in her father. Rolfe was safe—and this may have been the first time that she had felt this quality in a man. Smith and her father were volatile, but Rolfe was even. When he had trouble growing his tobacco, he let her teach him in the green rows. He was unique. He valued what she thought and, of more importance, he listened to her and respected her; his adoration was continuously fresh—and this time she was not a little girl. With what seems to be a sweeping transference, she found in Rolfe something akin to what she had found in Smith. Rolfe did something that Smith had not done, however; he spoke of something mysterious in her that he valued—her soul. As the weather warmed, they grew closer.

Then word came from the fort in March 1614. Negotiations for her release were about to begin.

When had he fallen in love with her? Was it in that blink when he saw her in the church, lit from the side by the small window? Was it in the way that she continually looked at him with deep and steady eyes as only his wife had looked at him? The intimacy of teaching and learning let them become close. In his own crisis, he was obsessed with her, but could he marry her? She was not English, nor even yet a Christian, and dealing with Dale could be a nightmare. He could not admit he wanted to marry her for his own personal reasons, Dale would never permit it. He had to propose the marriage as a business idea. Therefore, before he, Pocahontas, Dale, and a retinue of men set sail up the York toward Matchcut, Powhatan's new town, Rolfe wrote a letter, and waited.

The negotiations that April began with killings. A "great bravado" went up the shores from Indians demanding to know why they had come, adding they would do to them as they had to Ratcliffe. The English bellowed back, they had brought Pocahontas. Along the York, Indians fired arrows, the English returned shots, and as a result, villages burned and men died. The English were satisfied—for the second or third time—that they had avenged the killing of Ratcliffe and his men. When they reached Matchcut, some 400 armed warriors stood on the west bank of the river. They invited the English to come into the town, if they dared.

The English went ashore; warrior and solider alike moving face to face in lethal proximity, the Indians asked for the English werowance, to know why they were there. Although the fighting on the river was attributed to erring Indians, tension ran hot on both sides. They made a deal not to fight until noon the next day, and to negotiate before then, if possible. Two of Pocahontas's brothers demanded to see their sister. They had heard she was well, yet expected to see her in bad condition. She was well. And they "much rejoiced" upon seeing her there on shore, Hamor writes, and said that they would persuade their father to "redeem" her and make a lasting peace. She may have told them of her intention to marry an Englishman. Rolfe and Sparkes went to Powhatan to tell them their business, but he would not meet with them; they met with Opechancanough instead. Not ones to leave any ambiguity in mind, the English promised that, since they were here instead of planting corn, they would return, take their corn, burn their villages, and kill all their people if possible, if this deal did not go through. Hamor gave Rolfe's letter to Dale. Dale read it and his desire to kill and burn mellowed.

At noon the next day, Pocahontas went ashore with an English entourage to meet with her father. She strode confidently through the hundreds of people to the center of town, where Powhatan sat waiting, wearing his ceremonial cloak of deerskin studded with shells.

Pocahontas then made the most incredible speech that never was written down.

In essence, she spoke not only to her father but also to all the gathered Powhatan, who stood in the sunshine and listened to her speaking unfamiliar challenges in her still familiar voice.

Dale recorded that "The King's daughter went ashore, but would not talk to any of them, scarce to them of the best sort, and to them only that if her father had loved her, he would not value her less than old swords, pieces, or axes; wherefore she would still dwell with the Englishmen, who loved her." Pocahontas then turned on her heel and walked back through the deafening silence, amid the stir of moving heads, and reboarded the ship.

Rolfe, witness to the speech, pressed through the crowd of bodies, got on board the ship, and spoke to Dale, who promised formal permission to marry Pocahontas, in effect, for the sake of the colony. His letter emphasized how their marriage would be good for business, growing tobacco and converting Indians to Christianity. On the spot, Dale consented—and Rolfe proposed. The willowy young man asked her to marry him, and she said, "Yes."

A runner rushed back up the path into the confusion and relayed the news to the chief, who in his moment of loss simply acquiesced—whatever she wanted now, she could have. He hadn't

meant to lose her over swords; he didn't even care about them, they were just trophies. She was always a willful child and as a woman still more assertive. Powhatan gave her his blessing. That afternoon was the last time that father and daughter saw each other.

Dale was so overjoyed with developments, that sometime later he asked a runner to see if Powhatan would let him marry his other daughter—a girl of nine! No, Powhatan thundered; he had lost one daughter to the English; that was enough. Besides, she was promised in marriage to another chief.

Back in Jamestown, an enormous contingent of colonials and Indians—a few family members sent by Powhatan as emissaries— gathered in the church to see the blessed event of April 5, 1614. Light filled the church; in famous images, it shines on her alone, as a newly found Christian, while the Indians around her remain in the shadows. She wore what Smith described as "a tunic of Dacca muslin, a flowing veil and long robe of rich material from England." The marriage was complete and with it came eight years of peace, as Powhatan swore to bring an end to any and all hostility against the colonials—now that his daughter's life might be in jeopardy. Over time, he sent others to speak to her, and the answer they got was that she was "contented," which is bland enough to say almost nothing. When Powhatan asked Hamor how she was and got the same answer, his response was singular. He burst out laughing. If anyone knew his daughter, and her tormented affairs with happiness, he did.

Dale was more than happy, however; he wrote of how good fortune showered upon the colonists: their crops of corn and tobacco flourished; they hunted deer with impunity, without attack; and he alluded that the "God of battles"—meaning Okeus, perhaps—had taken the English side. Indeed, if success were the product of *manitu*, Pocahontas may have helped transplant that spirit into the colony. She literally helped Rolfe seed their new identity.

The peace was a dangerous condition, as Powhatan likely knew; it tipped the balance of power unfavorably away from him. The Chickahominy, barely allies of his, saw the shift and immediately came to an agreement with the English, in which they figured Powhatan as their enemy; other tribes followed. The paramount chief was now seen to be weak, and it didn't look to the other tribes as though he would be replaced anytime soon with his more aggressive brother.

During those peaceful years, the English flooded up the James River, not only physically but also psychologically. Their possession of the New World flourished in their imaginations and became their first call to empire; other colonies around the world would follow. The peace was as catastrophic to the Powhatan nation as it was beneficial to the English. The nation's roughly 15,000 native people, when Smith arrived, were displaced by 15,000 English in twenty years— one and all they came in through the wide and tranquil passageway that came to be known as the Peace of Pocahontas.

But if Pocahontas was contented, how happy was she? She had begun to find her individuality with Smith, and pursued this quest to the detriment of all she had known and loved. Rolfe had offered her everything she had not known, but she had also reacted to circumstances, and safe men can be dull men. As an appropriate man of God, was Rolfe more wan and passionless than she may have noticed, more inert than safe, more in love with his booming tobacco business than he was with her?

She helped him succeed, teaching him native methods of nurturing and cultivating tobacco. Although tobacco

was exclusively cultivated by Powhatan men, for religious reasons, she had learned enough through observation to instruct him in particulars like using a southern exposure and fish for fertilizer. Was he all about business now? In their time of short, practical lives, would love have mattered?

After a few extraordinary months in which she had felt her passions for Smith revive, she may have seen them die among the quiet coals of this man's hearth. Her pursuit of individuality had brought her to this point, still estranged from her people, though a few may have attended her in Henricus. Yet she was not close with anyone around her, and possibly lonely in her marriage. She had created her own life, but was now shackled from here to the afterlife—more hemmed and suffocated with propriety than she could have feared. Freedoms she had known with her people were not allowed. The emotional and sexual expressions so openly enjoyed among her people were sinful, even with her husband, and so all that was natural to her affectionate nature was evil, and cut her away from herself. She was growing not into herself in this new world, as she may have hoped, but away from herself. It was a tragic consequence that her father may have imagined, and one to which she was reconciled, under the banality of "contented." The young bride who had been so spirited was seen once again as a pensive woman, more solitary than social.

But here she was, and now she had a baby boy, Thomas. She had been christened herself. The girl who had been named Matoaka, who had taken on the spiritual name of Amonute, and who had become Pocahontas, her father's pet name, was renamed Rebecca. In May 1616, after two years of marriage, she and Rolfe went to London. She was nineteen and her legend would bloom.

In political terms, the English would exploit her as an example of the Good Indian, as someone who had renounced her culture for theirs, for its multiple layers of superiority, from technology to salvation. Still more deeply, though, the English imagination would see in the outline of her life the resolution of chaos that they called comedy: the grand coming together of disparate societies to fashion a still unimaginable future society on the foundations of the old. The rising Anglo population in Virginia would later embrace her story and Smith's as a grammar of the myths that they loved.

The landscape bristled. The coach rambled through meadows and over creeks, and the passengers were astonished to see the abundance. Uttamatomakkin looked across the jouncing interior at Pocahontas, who was then in her role and costume as Lady Rebecca; he may have remarked on all the corn and trees, having supposed the English were bereft of both. And there were so many people. Not long before they had departed for London, Powhatan had given the shaman and adviser a stick upon which he was to make a mark for every Englishman he saw to count the population. They were not even off the boat in Plymouth that day of June 3, 1616 when his work became too much. In the cast and call of docking, men in the riggings and on the pier, he threw the stick away. There were too many to count, which was bad news for the Powhatan: if the English had corn and trees and so many people, then their mission was not just to feed themselves and build houses, but to expand, forever.

Lady Rebecca may have been pensive on the carriage ride. In conversation, she must have learned that she was to inspire the Crown and the crowd to take a livelier interest in the colony, which, in spite of its new ramping exports in tobacco, was languishing financially. She was to present the new face of what the English saw as the noble creatures of her father's nation, and show that Christendom was now as viable as the rage for tobacco—Rebecca, formerly Pocahontas, was proof that this brave new world of their making would be a happy unity of mind, spirit, and business. The coach crested a rise in the road, and she saw London.

As an Indian woman who had grown up with no visual training in the matrix of abstractions that cities form, there is no way to know what her first impressions were. From her pious husband, though, she had learned a great deal of heaven and hell, and may have gleaned as well some of the infernal imagery of the Renaissance era. Tens of thousands of chimneys pumped black into the day, which hung in a smoky mass over the confusion of cobble and brick. Accustomed to a woodland empire, abreast with sunshine and rivers, paths and animals, and a language of solitude and signs, she was assaulted by the sights and sounds of London: the moiling of the industrial dark, of ashen figures thronging alongside their coach, the cramp and damp of quarters that blocked the sky, bloated faces, and air malodorous of horse dung. Her husband's smile of wan reassurance and the press of his hand on hers offered her little. Pale of comfort and pale of heart, he was with her. After they arrived and were welcomed at the modest boarding house, which the Virginia Company had penuriously reserved for them for the duration of their stay in London, Lady Rebecca at last

spoke to Uttamatomakkin, in private. See what you can find out, she said; John Smith—does he live?

More than seven years had passed since she had seen him; she had converted, married, and had a child, yet she still wanted to know. She did not know that Smith was alive and had played a part in ensuring she and her family were well accommodated. The inn the Rolfes were staying at was not the best place in London, but it was not the rancid establishment that the Virginia Company had planned to put them in. Smith had acted peremptorily once

again, mounting another campaign, this time on her behalf. When Smith had learned that Pocahontas was coming over with her new husband, he knew exactly how the Virginia Company would treat them. He made enquiries and discovered that the Rolfes' intended lodgings were miserable. He wrote immediately to the company, demanding that the company lodge them decently or face public embarrassment. Once that was done, Smith did something even more arrogant and audacious.

Sometime in early 1616, as a private citizen, he wrote a letter to Queen Anne. This now famous missive entreats the queen to give Pocahontas an audience, and to treat her with the same royal regard that she would any princess of European blood. He lists the many fine reasons why this exemplary young woman deserved such recognition: she had saved the colony on numerous occasions; she was the first Indian to be baptized a Christian and to speak English, to marry an Englishman and to bear him a child. To treat her as a peer of the Crown would further smooth relations with the Powhatan. This flood of adulation alone makes the letter interesting, but the letter probably would be no more than a footnote to history were it not for Smith's opening words. He reveals the reason why he always reacted to Pocahontas with such intensity and obligation— and though it would not be published for the public until 1624, the legendary tale of her rescue here meets the page for the first time. At last, he had his chance to be the great explorer. For Smith, only his ultimate reader, the Queen, could compel such such a confession from him. Given the way he doles out blame and credit equally in his writings, the chance that he now presented himself to the Queen with a stunning falsehood seems unlikely.

> "...if ingratitude be a deadly poison to all honest virtues, I must be guiltie of that crime if I should omit any meanes to bee thankful, So it is,
>
> That some ten yeeres agoe being in Virginia, and taken prisoner by the power of Powhatan their chiefe King, I received from this great Salvage exceeding great courtesies, especially from his sonne Nantaquaus, the most manliest, comeliest, boldest spirit, I ever saw in a Salvage, and his sister Pocahontas, the Kings most deare and welbeloved daughter, being but a childe of twelve or thirteene years of age, whose compassionate pitifull heart, of my desperate estate, gave me much cause to respect her: I being the first Chritian this proud King and his grim attendants ever saw...at the minute of my execution, she hazarded the beating out of her owne braines to save mine, and not onely that, but so prevailed with her father, that I was safely conducted to James towne...."

At court, Smith's letter and his story of having been saved circulated among advisers and royals alike, including King James, Queen Anne, and many other powerful figures in their circle. They knew of Smith. His letter published in 1608, *A True Relation*, which described in great detail the exploring he had done in Virginia, had given him both a professional and literary reputation in London. No one among the Queen's court questioned Smith's account of Pocahontas's role in his rescue, and it seems hardly likely that Smith would have laid his reputation out for public sacrifice on a lie. In

his own imperative tense, to credit and discredit everyone who deserved it, he politely beseeched the Queen to welcome a young woman whom he could never thank enough. If the rescue never happened, as many people nowadays believe, then it is a strange story to concoct after seven years—to thank her for nothing.

Some scholars allege that Smith was using Pocahontas to gain entrance to the royal court, so that he could meet the Queen and further his career; however, at the time Smith wrote the letter, he expected to be at sea when Pocahontas arrived in England, and therefore would miss any meeting. The Puritans had applied to lay a colony in the northern sweep of Virginia, an area that Smith had explored and had named New England; his first choice of name for Cape Anne was Cape Trabigzanda, honoring the Turkish noblewoman who had saved him. They needed a competent man to lead the expedition and Smith anticipated receiving the post; though, for some reason, Smith lost the commission to Miles Standish. (In 1620, when the expedition finally set sail, Standish missed the New York area and foundered on a formation called Plymouth Rock, where he planted the Puritans upon an inhospitable landscape. And though the people of Jamestown had a thanksgiving first, the Puritans would appropriate the renown for the event, and leave nothing to Jamestown but its ungrounded legends of Smith and Pocahontas.)

Although the young Indian woman was Lady Rebecca by title, she was Pocahontas in the brilliant season of 1616.

She was famous for being famous. The English had seen other Indians, but she was a multicultural picture of the American future, and in her adorable son, not yet two with black-black hair and eyes and coppery skin, the English could see a confluence of possibilities. This image of her, though, would be used against her people. As proof of English superiority in all things cultural, many people would point to her marriage as a de facto renunciation of her people and home culture, and see in her an exemplar of the Good Indian—the one who could be trained, civilized, housebroken, and recast into Anglo-Christian subservience. She was not that person, and the estrangement with her father two years earlier had not entailed a denunciation of her people. But the English used her that way—as would the Americans for centuries to come. That may explain why her life story, though complex and moving, is always reduced to saving Smith, as though without it, she would merit no biography of her own.

Dale had brought her to London to promote the colony, but her role in Jamestown's tobacco economy was central. Pocahontas used her skills of discernment and knowledge of farming and nurturing tobacco—learned amid the leafy rows with her mother—to help her husband grow into a wealthy planter. They named their Henrico farm Varina after Rolfe's new hybrid tobacco plant, which had become so popular that everyone in Jamestown was growing tobacco in lanes and yards for export to England. She had helped Rolfe to flourish, planting with her hands the Indian spirit of success into the otherwise flailing and failing enterprises of Jamestown, which even then was still on its way to bankruptcy. As she had saved Smith and his crew by giving them the Biblical equivalent of fish, now she saved the colony in perpetuity by teaching them, in Biblical terms, *how* to fish. With Rolfe's help, she had created a new tribe for herself; yet, this tribe was built around a product, not a community, foreshadowing however tenuously our own modern communities fashioned around a brand. Tobacco was the forerunner of tea and other English addictions that drove colonization, and Rolfe's successful entrepreneurship would

point to a new kind of business, where corporations rather than kings would make nations. Commercial exploitation of her image, beginning in the 19th Century, would drain her biography of her identity.

In spring of 1616, sitting in her writing room, bathed in the afternoon light, Queen Anne decided that she would meet with Lady Rebecca after all. She sent for the Rolfes to come to Whitehall. That late summer, the Rolfes brought their entire entourage of twelve Powhatan Indians, including her sister, Matachanna, wife of the shaman, to meet the Queen.

As a child, Pocahontas had charmed the English with her liveliness, turning cartwheels around the fort; now as a grown woman, she charmed them with her poise and reserve—everything original and lively about her was subsumed into English rectitude and bound by sartorial propriety. She was Lady Rebecca, not Pocahontas. She was powdered, piled, stuffed, stitched, sewn, and composed into a confection of Christian counterfeits. Even so, for all her new airs upon her entrance, her native athleticism and upbringing as a girl and woman of the woods showed in her weightless stride. She stood erect, confident, and deeply at ease with who she was—because she was self-invented. All about in the beams of light that slanted across the room were the lords and ladies who stood in judgment of her. There is no way to know what impressions Pocahontas drew of the men and women around her, though caricatures may suffice: doughy, pale and pasty, with bad skin and rotten teeth, unwashed, malodorous, and puffed with perfume to better mask the reality of filth fluffed in finery and feathers. In that summer hour, upon a moment's long entrance, Lady Rebecca owned their attention, as she came at last into the presence of the pale Majesty enthroned in the satin and squalor of the high Renaissance. She was about to win the hearts of a few men, and the condescension of them all. Her majesty, in powder and rouge, squinted at her from the throne above—with a mind to assess this singular new Christian.

The Queen saw that Rebecca was favored with good looks and fine skin, and that she was a fascinating contrast to those in her entourage. Rolfe was in demeanor a dull planter, but in the rear was Uttamatomakkin, in black and red paint, feathers, and deerskin, presenting all that was wild, or had been, in Lady Rebecca. The collective crowd saw in Rebecca the contrast and the continuity: the future of cultural blending that would transform the New World. Following the success of her royal presentation, invitations to famous parties ensued—the most famous was the Twelfth Night masque, a royal extravaganza of music, poetry, recitals, and comedy in honor of the king's lover, George Villiers. The Rolfes went to that and other parties and masques as ambassadors of Jamestown, raising its profile among potential investors, and enjoying the celebrity that had begun with her kidnapping three years earlier. For years, before her arrival, she had been famous as the nonpareil of her people, stemming from *A True Relation*. Now, she presented herself "as a Daughter of a King," at the Bishop of London's soiree, and the rising flow of respect was one that mutually increased her own status and that of her husband. Men, including Smith, wrote that she was the loveliest and most elegant lady of every great room she was in, and that her natural superiority to all those around her was instantly visible to anyone in her company. Some of her original animation ran playfully along in her conversation, and the men said that she was as witty and charming as she was lovely—though the veteran snob Ben Jonson lampooned her for not being "fair," meaning pretty and light skinned.

She was the guest of the season.

Everyone had to know her and to have an opinion, a moment to remember, a word of this and that which was theirs exclusively. The members of society wanted her to remember them, they wanted that flush of intimacy no one else could rival or claim, some angle that no one shared. No social season in London would be complete without an evening at the theater, and the Rolfes may have attended a 1616 production of Shakespeare's play, *The Tempest*.

The Globe roared with the voices of hoi polloi and high society alike, and it is tempting to imagine the Rolfes seated high above the commoners in a seat not far from Queen Anne and King James. This new production of the 1611 comedy was exhilarating. The playwright had found his inspiration in stories of the New World. He is thought to have read, as many had, William Strachey's account of the *Sea Venture*'s crash landing on Bermuda. Strachey loved theater and two or three times a week he went to productions at the Blackfriars Theater, which staged Shakespeare's plays, and where he hung out back stage. The two men had another connection in Shakespeare's sponsor, the Earl of Southhampton, who was also an avid supporter of the colony. Beyond these points of contact, the writer quite possibly also had heard hearsay that had circulated out of the royal court—like the story in Smith's letter to Queen Anne of a princess saving his life. He may have heard the story in 1611, from Smith himself in a literary pub, or have read the account by the Spanish soldier saved in Florida. While the rescue may have struck the playwright as twaddle, its other elements of story, characters and hurricane, clearly inspired in him the conceit of a satiric comedy.

One point is tantalizing, though—the likeness that some scholars see between the songs of the character Ariel and the dances of the Algonquin Indians of Virginia. By 1611 only one man might have complained in London pub braggadocio of "being tormented" by dancing women and girls. So there may have been at least one conversation between the two men—or a moment when Shakespeare listened to Smith.

Shakespeare's language was difficult for Lady Rebecca, but she would have understood the outline of the play. She and her husband may have been stunned by the resemblances to their lives. If some aspects were familiar, others of a deeper nature might have called out to them, also. These guide us to an aquifer of mythos from which readers of the play will draw the continuing vivacity of Pocahontas and Smith as characters for centuries.

The Tempest tells the story of a powerful magician, Prospero, who lives in exile from his homeland with Miranda, his spirited but naïve daughter, on the island of Bermuda. They have a slave, Caliban, a half-man creature who is deformed, born of a witch and the sea. Prospero longs to return to his homeland of Milan and rule again as a Duke. To deal with his enemies, who exiled him to the island, he sends a huge hurricane down upon their nearby ship and brings it crashing onto the island; a few survivors wander ashore—and at the sight of Ferdinand, a young lord, Miranda becomes flush with innocent passion. Miranda begs her father not to kill him, to

let her have him. Prospero grants her wish, with complications. Slave and slave owner hate each other, and to gain power as an equal to Prospero, Caliban, who once tried to rape Miranda, plots to kill his master. At the end of the play, all intrigues are forgiven and harmony restored. Caliban, vanquished by Prospero, finds himself ensnarled with Prospero in the past; while Miranda—whose innocence plays into her name, which suggests looking without seeing—marries Ferdinand and together they create a new society of the future.

While *The Tempest* has enjoyed centuries of analysis from an English view, and often seen as his American play, we might swing it round and view its dramaturgy fully from Powhatan shores,

which is necessarily hypothetical but intriguing. If one can see some resemblance between Miranda and Prospero to Pocahontas and Powhatan, who made all things happen mysteriously in the forest, was guided by his shaman, and voiced a lamenting desire to return to his homeland—a pre-invasion state of normality—then we can easily see in Ferdinand first a likeness to Smith, which then gives way to the probable Rolfe.

But how does Smith fit into this template? The convention today is to portray Caliban as an African or a South American Indian—indeed, sometimes as a revolutionary—to put the play on a neocolonial stage. Some scholars see in the character of Caliban a melding of the European "wild man" and the Virginia Native Americans. This view presents "natural" people—first Indians and later Africans—as dehumanized individuals who must be civilized by Europe. This take on the play would be a liner note if not for the fact that precisely such thinking rationalized the treatment of indigenous and African peoples in Virginia for centuries. Just as renaissance ideas were in the atmosphere in the founding of the Virginia Company, so, too, were tacit ideas of class and race, savagery and success, as the colony grew larger.

If one can suppose, however, that Caliban is half human because he is half-civilized and half-barbaric, then his birth from the wood and water is a mythic representation. Caliban comes out of the water and lives in the woods; he is hotly reactive; he cannot control his mood swings; his only passion is to kill Prospero; he cannot feed himself, or speak the language; he lusts after Miranda, and describes her as a "nonpareil"—it could be said that Caliban resembles Smith. While this reading may seem out beyond anomalous, one needs to remember that Shakespeare was not one to insult his patrons, but to lampoon the Queen and court by sly misdirection and euphemism—seen this broadly, in his satirizing of English imperialism, Caliban embodies England, a childish and childlike neophyte among the more sophisticated colonial nations.

Miranda cries, "Oh, brave new world that has such people in it!" To which Prospero dourly mutters, "'Tis new to thee." The old man, not unlike Powhatan, has seen more of the world and expects a great deal less of it, and though he is happy to return home, he is now always stuck with Caliban. The very centerless form of this enchanted colonial comedy emulates the whirling of a hurricane, a social vortex from which only a few escape—into the past or future.

On this apocryphal evening, it is tempting to imagine John Smith shifting uneasily as he watched the play, feeling an acute discomfort at something he cannot name. He would not have seen himself in Caliban, but in Ferdinand. To him, Pocahontas was recognizable in Miranda, yet it was Shakespeare who had swooped down and written about her. *That* was his story, or it could be if he wrote it. Smith actually had known her, but Shakespeare had placed her into a luminous work of art, while Smith had only his journalistic letters and hyperbole. So, it may be that *The Tempest*, inspired by the *Sea Venture*'s misadventures, later inspired Smith to pull Pocahontas out of memory, name her, and give her a place in his story and in our history.

All of which would mean that the story of Smith and Pocahontas, as a story, had drawn upon a reservoir of the unconscious, the same dream-logic that makes the *Tempest* the masterpiece it is. It broadens the characters into archetypes and the narrative into an essential grammar in which stories of an emerging self are written in the West, as they have been back to Greek antiquity. The comedy promises an allegorical new society for a new nation. Whether Smith was inspired to write his own version, or defend her against snobs, his tale of Pocahontas would live on for those looking for a secular saint and a story that would canonize her virtue—and in some oblique way, reflect their own.

Lady Rebecca was coughing,

and before the play was over, her husband decided to take her home. The tickle in her throat that had plagued her for some time was worse, having moved into her chest, and she may have seen spots of blood in her linen handkerchief. Even some members of her entourage had begun to cough—including Matachanna, who had come along to be her son's nanny, and young Thomas. They may have contracted pneumonia or tuberculosis; a child of smoky houses, she would have been susceptible to both. Spring was approaching. Rolfe moved his family out of London's heavy air and into the town of Brentford in the hope that, here in the country miles from London, Rebecca and the others would recover their health before they set sail to the colony in March. Here they walked outside and could feel the light in the trees once again, and some thought she revived a bit. With the progression of her illness, Rebecca had grown pensive again, though she may have had an old obsession on her mind—someone she had not yet seen.

But the shaman had seen him. Uttamatomakkin encountered Smith at a grand masque, where there was much dancing and drinking. He complained to Smith that he still had not met the King, who had been absent when they went to see Queen Anne. Smith assured him that he had—the king was the shriveled and dirty little man he had met earlier that night. The shaman was stunned—*that* was the king? He asked Smith, Why can't East and West be friends and trade as equals? Smith could not answer him, and he was agonized by the man's next words: "You gave Powhatan a white Dog, which Powhatan fed as himselfe, but your King gave me nothing, and I am better than your white Dog." After such an unhappy conversation, the shaman might have simply forgotten to tell Pocahontas about Smith.

Smith had been thinking about her, too, but he was now a Captain without a commission, and like many men he felt an acute embarrassment over his lack of success and stature. He had been a big man in her father's world; here he was a nobody, and he was susceptible to feeling the want of such measurements. She may have transformed Rolfe but not him. Even so, Smith could not postpone his temptation another week, so one day, he rode out impulsively—without even a letter of hello—to Brentford to see the woman, her husband, and the life she was sharing with another man. The visit may have been in summer, only months after they arrived, happening on an unspecified day.

The Rolfes were inside, expecting no one, when he arrived. Rolfe rose to speak to the butler, who informed them of a visitor. By the time Rebecca had set her book down and also risen, Smith was at the threshold of the room. The shock of seeing him was too much for her: the nearly eight years since she last saw him entirely dissolved, and so did she. Lady Rebecca fell away and Pocahontas stood there.

She faintly said hello, seemed pensive, and suddenly turned her face away. She left the two men and went to her room. Closing the door, she then wept with so much emotion that Smith and Rolfe sat and listened to her sobbing down the hall. Pocahontas did not weep lightly or briefly, but as a woman and girl who had loved this man, had lived on without him in a state of high ambiguity over whether he was alive, and had married a man who might well have been a wan substitute. Faced with the power and confusion of her emotions, the men must have waited in an equally stoic awkwardness. She did not come back. Pocahontas wept for two to three hours. When she did return, she was Lady Rebecca once again—and she was politely if coldly formal, more English than Smith.

Her first question was direct: Why didn't you tell me you were alive?

Smith demurred. Over there I was someone; here I'm no one. I didn't want you to see that.

And do you think that is what mattered to me? Pocahontas said in her Lady Rebecca manner. That's what I care about? Your status?

In their volley, volumes are left unsaid. For an acknowledged braggart, Smith's concession of his status is extraordinary—but not as much as his concession that it mattered so much to him what she would think of him now, to see him as a plain man. Just as remarkable is that she is frankly exasperated that he would think—even for a moment—that she could be so shallow. It was him she wanted to see, but just as he failed to understand that the night she had warned him and his fifteen men, and he had given her the blue glass beads, here she was once again, trying to make him understand.

In his *General History,* Smith lets her speak for herself. Hers is an unforgettable intelligence and this voice is hers forever.

Smith writes, "she began to talke, and remembered me well what courtesies shee had done: saying, 'You did promise Powhatan what was yours should be his, and he the like to you; you called him father being in his land a stranger, and by the same reason so must I doe you.'"

Smith cannot let her show him such an honor, however. "I durst not allow of that title, because she was a King's daughter; with a *well set countenance* [emphasis mine] she said, 'Were you not afraid to come into my fathers Countrie, and caused feare in him and all his people (but mee) and feare you here I should call you father; I tell you then I will, and you shall call mee childe, and so I will bee forever and ever your Countrieman.'"

She later states, "They did tell us always you were dead, and I knew no other till I came to Plimoth; yet Powhatan did command Uttamatomakkin to seeke you, and know the truth, because your Countriemen will lie much."

With her face set, she upbraided him for not having approached her, for not allowing her to show him an honor of her people by calling him father, simply because he wasn't a king himself. She solidified this new understanding between them by demanding that he always show her the filial honor of calling her child—and then she swore to an undying allegiance with him. For those people who insist Smith and Pocahontas were no more than acquaintances, no sense of having profoundly influenced one another, this behavior is simply inexplicable. After almost eight years of not having seen one another, the bond is still so evocative that, even if it does not entail several rescues, it involves a love caught somewhere between that of a father and daughter and lovers—in perpetuity.

Whatever the reasons for their frustration, they remain in a romantic embrace in which lovers are perpetually frozen before a kiss, untainted by life and death. What is finally most moving in this scene is that it follows upon her new understanding of a life after death, in Christian terms. When she swears to be his countryman forever and ever, she is making a vow with him, not of marriage, but to be with him in some way and as close as they would ever be, in an everlasting life.

AN ENORMOUS WAVE OF

MIGRATION

DROVE THE ENGLISH IN GREAT NUMBERS ACROSS THE ATLANTIC

ULTIMATELY BRINGING AN END

TO THE POWHATAN EMPIRE.

LEST A TWIG SHOULD BREAK AND EVERYONE CRY

Powhatan came to the deerskin flap of his house.

John Rolfe stood there. No account exists of their conversation, but it was not a happy one.

Pocahontas's cough had worsened by the time they had to sail for Virginia, and as the ship drew abreast of the Atlantic, Rolfe was desperate to get her help; though not much more than thirty years old, he had already lost a wife and daughter. He convinced the ship's captain, Samuel Argall, the same man who had kidnapped Pocahontas years earlier, to steer the ship back to the town of Gravesend. They installed her comfortably at an inn, but no prayers or doctor would hold her long in this world. She had lived four lives by then, the doorway to each marked by a new name, and in her voice at the end, you hear resignation, perhaps mixing the stoicism of her people with the afterlife beliefs of her adopted people. Having rescued so many errant men in her brief life, she continued to care for her husband, telling him not to grieve or worry. "All men die," she said, "'tis enough that the child liveth."

Rolfe buried her in the nave of a nearby church, and she was later moved outside under the shade trees in the churchyard—a statue there marks the end of the path that she followed one day, as a girl, to the fort.

What of young Thomas? Although her sister and the others were on the mend, the two year old remained very sick; in a state of grief and, perhaps, confusion, Rolfe left Thomas in the care of his brother. Rolfe would not see Thomas again: He returned to the Jamestown colony, remarried, and died of unknown causes in 1622, cast into an unmarked grave.

Many scholars today consider Pocahontas to have been a child who contributed no more than a pretty fairy tale to the history of her time, denying her any historic individuality, intelligence, or awareness of how her estrangement and marriage were exploited. The real politics of her time belie such a dismissive evaluation. She knew and she saw, and her pain of loss was always evident, as her afternoon with Smith in England shows. She had seen her father bestow peace on the colony, and his gift was the last and ineluctable outcome of the small ways in which she had challenged him all her life by intervening and saving someone set for execution, English and Indian alike. Others exploited her individuality to survive, and eventually to ruin the Powhatan—but that was a tragedy beyond her influence or desire.

When he heard the news of his daughter's death, Powhatan was living on the northern border of his nation along the Potomac. Anticipating the rising English invasion, he had left Werowocomoco. Powhatan's relocation of the seat of Powhatan government from a place twenty miles from the English to the nation's extreme opposite border, and that much closer to the southern tribes of the Iroquois, longtime Powhatan enemies, alarmed his brothers. When the English had arrived a decade earlier, his coalition was on a path to a state of permanency in field and architecture. Now the English threat had caused the Powhatan to revert to previous ways. Powhatan's withdrawal threatened the shape of the chiefdom; the consequences were more than disquieting among his people.

But if Powhatan were able to still move about geographically as a tactician, his son-in-law told him a truth that day in 1617 that pinned him to his old age. He had sent his young daughter to the colonial fort with the result that she married an Englishman and brought about a peace during which he had lost the nation. Some losses are compound, others mortally wounding, and the eloquence of his loss lies quietly in the fact that nothing is known of his last year. He did not see the English again, and he died at age eighty less than a year after his daughter.

When Powhatan had told Hamor in 1614 that too many of their people had died and it was time for peace, the Chief must have known, as an astute politician, that his final acquiescence to his daughter to hold onto her might undermine his authority within the volatile factions of his coalition. Nevertheless, like many a father who feels the acute loss of a daughter's love, he may have decided that he could do it all, and that national solidarity was not at risk. He was wrong.

The old man passed quietly from power; his brothers would not follow his example. Opechancanough stepped into power along with Opitcham, who was physically lame and inclined to let Opechancanough lead the way. They had seen the power shift among the Indian tribes during the last six years of peace. The

Chickahominy had always been reluctant members of the coalition, and after the marriage of Pocahontas to an Englishman, they saw an English transcendence. They continued to pay a yearly tribute to Powhatan, but they signed a peace treaty with the English, acknowledging the Powhatan as their common enemy. Other strategists also maneuvered their factions around the large and amassing colonial threat.

The peace, presented along with Pocahontas's international celebrity, catalyzed the disasters of Jamestown and transformed the incompetent colony into a robust enterprise.

Pocahontas had helped Rolfe grow his hybrid tobacco, which made him rich and which also gave the colony a future, and by loose extension a future for colonization elsewhere. If Opechancanough thought he could drive the English out now, he was a decade too late.

Once the colony was thriving, the many fathers of its success took time to blame the man they most hated. In 1621, Smith found himself testifying before a commission in London established to find out what had gone so wrong in the colony that so many had died. Both enemies and allies listened to his testimony or later read transcripts. They denounced him for being vainglorious and responded loudly to the many accusations that peppered Smith's testimony—for instance, that his own men had drawn muskets on him after he had been blown up—but when Smith testified that Pocahontas was God's instrument in saving his life, no one laughed. Since they didn't attack, Ralph Hamor, Captain Samuel Argall, George Percy, Michael and William Fettiplace, and David Wyffin—brother of Richard, whom allegedly Pocahontas once saved—these notable men of the colony must have reluctantly believed him. The loudest silence comes from Captain West; Henry Spelman claimed that Smith had conspired with Powhatan to kill West; so if anyone had reason to denounce Smith, West did. None of the writings of these men corroborate Smith's story about Pocahontas, but none of them tell of his capture in the swamp, either. Considering that these men allegedly tried to kill Smith, and that they accused him of once trying to make himself king and of exaggerating his deeds, their silence speaks of collusion.

Beyond these men are many other colonials, as well as 200 Indian witnesses. Not one of them, English or Indian, dismissed the story. In the years and decades following the rescue scene, the story seems to have lived on in the oral tradition of Indian and English alike. The story deserves the same respect that other tales in that tradition receive—many of which are far more fantastic than this rescue.

Among those captivated by the story was Reverend Samuel Purchas, who had had the pleasure of meeting the tribal shaman Uttamatomakkin when he had accompanied Pocahontas to London. The reverend questioned the shaman about Okeus and other aspects of Powhatan religious life. The Indians were polytheistic and happy to learn of another god, but could not grasp the danger presented by an insecure and jealous god, who wants no others before him. To demonstrate how accessible Okeus was, the shaman conjured Okeus in the parlor and described him to the Englishman—tall, well made, and handsome, with hair falling down the left side of his head to the ground. There is

no account of the irony here that the god who had predicted the rise of a dangerous tribe in the bay was now visiting that tribe's home world. Intrigued, Reverend Purchas began to investigate the stories about Jamestown.

Very quietly, he asked the colonials about the Starving Time, the violence, and Chief Powhatan. And then he asked about the

singular story in which the girl, Pocahontas, had put her head over Smith's, risking her life to save his own. One and all simply responded that the girl was always at the fort, following Smith around; that he could have married her; and that they knew she had saved his life. Not one of them accused him of lying—rather they accused Smith of the reverse: of promoting himself, of talking about himself and telling his own stories, which affronted the self-effacing sensibility of the English.

Until the 1640s, Jamestown was a place out of time that would not exist again in America until the late twentieth century. A kind of spacious relational ease existed. With some eighty percent of the population indentured, whites and blacks, an air of tolerance existed that sometimes seems remarkably contemporary, even toward sexual identity. One man was given to wearing a dress one day and trousers the next. His frequent transitions alarmed and infuriated the men, but they simply demanded he choose a sex, it did not matter which, and stop going back and forth. Interracial marriages, though eventually prohibited, reflected the changing attitude toward slavery in England, where the practice was in the process of being abolished; conversely,

slavery would slowly take root in the James River plantations and become a legal institution in 1705.

In 1619, the tensions within Jamestown rose to the surface and became the main branches feeding American Identity. A signature event was the first convention of the House of Burgesses, with twenty-two members representing eleven plantations and, albeit indirectly, the future of American democracy. A Dutch man-o-war arrived in Jamestown that year as well, bearing twenty slaves. Although the slaves were destined for sale in the Spanish Caribbean, they were exchanged for food and supplies in Jamestown, where they worked in concert with farm owners in the tobacco fields and were treated as indentured servants.

Until the arrival of slaves, two temperaments had driven against one another in Jamestown. One mentality, augured and driven by Smith, demanded an individual self-sufficiency that leveled the classes. The mentality brought by lords and pursued by De Le Warr, Gates, Dale, and others brought forth a corporate economy, which bolstered the class structure. Smith had been outraged when only forty men worked to feed 150 people. That ratio was about to explode into a system of plantations. Built upon slavery and growing huge on international trade involving molasses and rum, these essentially feudal farms would institutionalize racism and genocide to enslave Africans and take Indian lands. Everything Smith had despised about his lazy lords was about to come into being in Virginia on the scale of an anti-utopian nightmare. The tensions of the individual and of the group, both felt and fought by Smith and Pocahontas, would play for centuries, and diffuse throughout American ideology.

An enormous wave of migration drove the English in great numbers across the Atlantic, ultimately bringing an end to the Powhatan Empire. The English population went from 450 in 1620 to roughly 4,500 people by 1622. The majority of the new arrivals, white and black, had chosen or had been sentenced to indentured servitude in place of prison time. Others were kidnapped while out

American Identity would flow not only with a corporate mentality, or that of self-sufficiency alone, but also with righteousness and rebellion against all kinds of tyranny. Seen from this vantage point, still within the first decades of the seventeenth century, it now appears that America's Civil War was the second act of the American Revolution—whose defining tension between the individual and the corporation had begun on that swampy little island. The rough parallel between the states' rights and the federal government's rights shows how Smith's individualism had twisted over a century into representing Virginia's First Families, who conflated his cause with theirs. They were using him; no wonder Adams and others tried to dismantle him. Smith would have hated them, their laissez faire grandeur, and their slavery. Yet, if we see the men behind the ideas of the individual and the company as Smith and Dale, then their conflicts and the War Between the States were wars of modernity that severed America at last from the long hand of medieval Europe.

Some of this complex history lived in a man who arrived in Jamestown in 1621 aboard the *James*. He was identified simply as "Antonio, a Negro"; his homeland is still unknown. Although many of the early Africans in the colony were indentured, Anthony was a slave. He was purchased to work on the large Bennett Plantation across the river from Jamestown. The owners of the thriving tobacco farm wanted to expand their range of products to include silk, iron, and glass. Traveling under the humid skies to the Bennett plantation, there is no telling what Anthony thought of his new condition or estate.

In the eight years since the Peace of Pocahontas, Virginia Company officials, such as Edwin Sandys, who had brought the Bennett family in as investors, thought that the colony was secure enough to expand its growth of plantations. To ensure the peace, the colonials went to new extremes in sensitivity: they opened their houses to the Indians, inviting them inside for a prayer or meal; they conspicuously killed dogs accused of barking at, biting, or

drinking in the pubs and were thrown onboard Virginia-bound ships. These people were known as "spirits," and their kidnappings may have inspired the phrase, "spirited away."

Indentured servants typically had to labor under a master for seven years to earn their freedom. At first, blacks and whites achieved their freedom equally, but by the 1630s the term of servitude for blacks had stretched into perpetuity. By the 1640s, many whites and blacks were so furious over their mistreatment that they joined together to fight their overlords. Laws were enacted to disarm the blacks, just as the English had tried to keep the Indians disarmed. But a common enemy had given the indentured servants, regardless of race or color, a common cause.

The burgeoning new tobacco economy and its evolving system of corporate plantations forced the English to consider slavery here even though the practice was then dying in England. The nascent capitalism would rise only on the backs of the indentured and the enslaved, engendering a sense of entrapment and futility that inspired so much fury in the colony. For the indentured and the enslaved, life in the colony was brutal. And in one current, frightening Indians. Regardless of these overtures, a Powhatan man known as "Jack of the Feathers"—so nicknamed for wearing swan's wings attached to his shoulders as though he could fly—continued to harass the colonials. They killed him in late 1621, unwittingly setting in motion a catastrophe that stole quietly toward them.

In the spring of 1622, nine hundred people lived up and down the James River on various grand and humble farms and plantations, clustered in villages of families, like the Flower Dew One Hundred, or solitary families living on isolated farms. Given the prevailing peace of the last couple of years, the colonials were lulled into an easy somnolence on the morning of March 22, 1622, when the axe fell. John Rolfe was likely still living on Varina, which faced the woodlands not far from Pocahontas' brother, Parahunt.

The morning began routinely:

workers toiled in the fields and houses were open to any visiting Indian. The Indians soon appeared. As usual, they carried no weapons and came across the fields with their hands open at their sides, a traditional show of welcome. But something was not right. At some houses, the Africans went to their masters and told them that the Indians were acting oddly. Their warnings were dismissed. At the Bennett Plantation, Anthony might have been outside when he saw what was happening. The Indians walked through the field, looked at him, and then vanished into the house. There may have been a war cry from the trees, the signal to attack: moments after the Indians entered the house, screams were heard.

In an echo of the warning from Pocahontas to Smith, the warriors lifted knives and tools and attacked their hosts at their meal, in the barn, wherever they were. The killing was quick but not clean—they disfigured the dead, taking scalps, noses, breasts, and "unspeakable" appendages (possibly meaning genitals). By noon, 350 people had been killed. Fifty-two people were killed on

the Bennett Plantation; among the few who escaped were Anthony and six others, slaves and servants, who had hid in terror of the Indians. Even if they had not hid, it is doubtful that they would have been killed: nowhere that day did an Indian kill an African; the Indians recognized another suffering tribe.

A little ways from the Bennett Plantation, an English family managed to escape the slaughter, as well; in a twist of fate reminiscent of Pocahontas's interventions, a young Indian boy named Chanko had run through the woods sometime earlier that morning to save them. Pocahontas was not the only youth to feel protectively toward a surrogate father figure among the English. Chanko had been raised by the English family, and loved the man who treated him like a son. While in the woods earlier that morning, Chanko had been recruited by the Indians to kill the family—instead, he ran and told his adoptive father. The man rowed across the James and warned the people of the fort, giving them an advantage when the Indians attacked. Today, Chanko's memory is problematic for the Virginia Indian community, but no one discredits the story; devoid of romance, the story draws no attacks. The appeal of legends, then,

may not be in the story structure but in the romanticism such a tale may elicit—not the sense, but rather the sensibility that arouses and then satisfies or irritates.

And though nothing is known exactly of how John Rolfe died, there is a temptation here to follow scholarly speculation that he may have died that day in the attack, and go a few steps further—that the men coming toward him with open hands were Pocahontas's brothers and her uncle, Opechancanough: a simple invention that shows the seductive symmetry and catharsis of myth.

After the attack, Opechancanough may have thought that his own brand of psychological warfare would mortify the English and send them home. He was wrong; by disfiguring the dead for trophies, the Indians actually galvanized English resolve. Opechancanough could not have foreseen the consequences; he was working from an old model: kill enough English and they'll retreat down the river and stay on the island. Had the Indians attacked when the colonials first landed in 1607, or even in 1610 during the Starving Time, the English might have left, but now they were deeply convinced Virginia was theirs. By 1622, he would have to have killed them all.

The English were quick to retaliate.

When the English and the Powhatan met shortly after the attack to sign a peace treaty, the English poured wine for everyone, raised a toast, and then stood back to watch. In the afternoon sun, some two hundred Powhatan men drank the poisoned wine, concocted by the colony's doctor, John Potts, and died in the shadow of the peace treaty they had just signed with the English, who "will lie much." The fifty who didn't die were butchered. If nothing else, this agreement was a harbinger of what was to come for the next four centuries. What began with that "peace" in the Powhatan forest would roll across the continent until the dead were beyond counting—on anyone's stick.

To a certain extent, Opechancanough's attack was inconsequential when one considers that a disease caused by spoiled imported beer hit the colony around the same time and truly devastated its population. Over the next couple of years, the colony's numbers dropped from about 4,500 to about 500. Even the indifferent King James had seen too many die; he disbanded the Virginia Company charter in 1624, made the colony a royal possession, and sent in the troops. Mayhem ensued. Indians were killed indiscriminately, without regard for tribe or treaty. Once aroused to a passion, the English could do this. They had subjugated many of the tribes around their home island—the Welsh, Irish, Scots, and others—and now they made America their new military frontier. Smith and Strachey had already likened the Indians to Britain's various tribes, and now the Powhatan would follow their fate as well. As Powhatan had miscalculated the English endurance in the beginning, so Opechancanough miscalculated their resolve at the end.

In London, Smith wrote furious articles in which he called for the decimation of the Indians. Various groups that wanted to send colonials to the New World all rejected him. For reasons that he could not fathom, they thought him a bad hire. He vented his frustrations on everyone by calling for revenge. He offered to return to the colony and lead the war. In spite of his antagonism toward the Powhatan, though, he was even then writing fondly of Pocahontas, her brother, and others who had been kind to him. In 1624, his first book, *A General History of Virginia*, appeared. It included the famous story of how Pocahontas risked her life to save his. In telling the tale, he does more than promote himself. He separates out an individual female for praise, while railing against her people, resolving a pair of contradictions by using romance to touch empathy. Americans would always show gratitude to other Indian women who helped white men, and shower affection upon remarkable individuals whose culture is one they also fear. Just such a narrative may be the vital link between hostile peoples who form a society, must eventually outlive their tragedies, and survive together.

The rescue story consists of little more than a sentence in Smith's writings. His life was about a lot more than that, and he made that point relentlessly for hundreds of pages. Pocahontas, the girl and the young woman, does appear in various other colonial accounts, though astonishingly, only in fourteen sentences—and in most of these, someone notes only that she was present. Smith alone admired her and gave her important space in their accounts.

The arc of Pocahontas's life is charted on only fourteen sentences. That may not seem a lot, but when we pause to think of how much we know of Shakespeare, for instance, it becomes a lot. Beyond Ben Johnson's poem and some reviews, no contemporary seems to have to written a line about Shakespeare the man, as Smith did about Pocahontas. It seems strange that this girl and woman, so lightly regarded now, garnered at the time far more biography than the most famous playwright of their age. Perhaps such a presence and influence reflects the time—when the English venerated strong women rulers. And Pocahontas was strong.

The nineteenth-century writers and poets who seized upon the rescue scene as the one in her life to emphasize have obscured her strength of character and resolve, and the sheer heartbreaking complexity of what she endured. Her pursuit of individuality represents that emerging, and now transcendent, part of American identity.

Jamestown was a thriving scene of plantations in 1635

when a young man came ashore and entered the fort. Thomas Rolfe was twenty-one years old, coppery in color, black of eyes and hair, and looked very much like his famous mother. His grandfather, Powhatan, had left him an inheritance of more

than a thousand acres around the remains of what had been the Powhatan coalition, Tsenacommacoh. With almost luxurious irony, Powhatan had made his grandson one of the richest men in the colony—giving him Indian lands to make him rich by English standards. Thomas became a wealthy planter, married Jane Poythress, and raised not only tobacco, but also legends of his own. The founding families of Virginia—Lees, Randolphs, and others—would trace their lineage back to their multicultural and multiracial ancestry, via Thomas, to Pocahontas and the Powhatan. As odd as this may seem in a section of the country infamous for racism, there lies in their claim an annealing awareness of the mosaic identity that springs from the native and foreign coalitions that clashed here. The deeper hybrid grown with sun and water was that of the myriad cultures, distinct yet combined, in Virginia.

The same year that Thomas Rolfe arrived, another man petitioned to buy 1,650 acres of land in Waresquioake County. His list of individuals who would be working the various parcels of land included the slave Anthony and his wife, Mary. Anthony had been lucky to marry. The colony had few women, and even fewer African women—and marriage with Indian women was still an anomaly. (The Indians actually considered it an insult that more of their women were not married to colonials.) Anthony and Mary eventually raised hogs and cattle, which were as vital an industry as tobacco, since the colonials had to eat. Anthony succeeded in purchasing his own freedom, and his wife's; he took the last name of Johnson. By the 1640s, his herds were growing and by mid-century he had become one of the colony's notable entrepreneurs. He bought his own land: His 250-acre holding along Pungoteague Creek was not as large as the greater plantations, but it was large by Eastern Shore standards; in the tragic economy of the era, he even owned his own African slaves. As the years passed, the political climate of the colony and its orbital plantations was shifting and dangerous. Slavery was advancing rapidly and peace with the Indians was unpredictable.

187

The clashes continued. In 1644, Opechancanough attacked again and another four hundred English were killed, but by this time the livelihood of the colony and its future were so secure that this attempt to rid the country of the English is almost forgotten. Opechancanough was an old man by then; he had seen the most incredible changes. He had seen his generations die out three times, when he was a youth; he might have been kidnapped, and seen the reach and homeland of the Spanish Empire; he had seen his brother hesitate, and his niece married; and he had met his English nephew, who was raising his family here. Tsenacommacoh was disappearing under the rising tide of colonials. Even the Chickahominy, who had struck a deal with the English to save themselves, were not safe from the English encroachment. And, in spite of his stature, neither was Opechancanough.

After the 1644 attack, Opechancanough was captured and brought to Jamestown. The town had grown over one end of the island. One day while walking about, he may have been looking about at the flux of change around him, remembering when the island was a swamp and death camp, or reliving his extraordinary life, or simply thinking of what he would have for dinner. He may have seen some ghost of the future in the brick row houses, the lanes, and yards, fences and faces. At the age of one hundred, he had seen everything and had anticipated every treachery, but not this one: a soldier shot him in the back. He fell and died, surrounded by English faces.

Some historians believe that history moves in waves, and others in particles. Waves centuries old had been pushing with unrelenting force on the Powhatan, but when Opechancanough died, they began dispersing as a people. A new chief negotiated peace with the English and then, all at once, the Powhatan began to fade—moving on, joining other tribes, but acting on the now unmistakable conclusion that their future had been written by their enemies.

For the Indians, English, and Africans, an evolving sense of identity reflected back onto the landowner from the emerging political and social landscape. Ownership entailed political rights and accomplishment engendered community respect. For those who owned and farmed their land, shaping the landscape within this new narrative grew a new identity. As habits became values, values became rights. America began growing in Indian soil.

The natural rights of Americans arose from land, accomplishment, and success—and one day would culminate in a pursuit of happiness. Against this new dynamic, the escalating loss of land was devastating to the Indians.

Their mobility changed from an ancient cultural practice into the flight of refugees. As they lost their land, so they began loosening the bonds of culture. The dominant new culture would reflect on them an identity of worthlessness. The destruction of Smith's terrorism was being written anew for new Indian generations, with consequences that still devastate First American communities into our time.

In 1646, the English, chastened by the sudden and utter clearing of the tidewater woods, began to create reservations for the Pamunkey, Chickahominy, and others who had once been part of the Powhatan coalition. The lines drawn were meant to allow the Indians to hold onto inherited land inside of an English legal system, so that others could not continue stealing more of what had already been stolen. The colonials also began to buy land from the tribes, a practice started by John Smith in his last weeks in Virginia—his idea for securing peace. Unfortunately, the idea did not work in the 1640s: ownership meant different things to each party—for instance, the Indians believed they had the right to hunt a herd on their former property—which led to fighting.

The historic moment for Jamestown was ending by the late seventeenth century. As many Indians left the tidewater area—as of 1669 there were only 1,800 Powhatans remaining—colonials began to abandon Jamestown, pushing deeper into the surrounding landscape. The end was precipitated by Nathaniel Bacon, who led raids against the indigenous people, and eventually against the English for an array of complaints about high taxes, low tobacco prices, and lack of protection against the remaining Indians. In 1676, Bacon burned Jamestown to the ground—and with it all documents that might have supported or contradicted legends. Despite the fact that Bacon died soon afterward, and his rebels—an assortment of whites and blacks—were hunted down, the Indian attacks ended completely. The tidewater region was now an English province.

Jamestown was rebuilt, but it did not survive.

Before the eighteenth century, even the English gave up on Jamestown and moved to Williamsburg, which was built on ground eighty feet higher and almost free of mosquitoes; architecturally, Williamsburg was an English outpost. In 1693 the College of William and Mary was founded, and the tidewater colonial world was intact. Each passing year brought more and more colonials to Virginia's shores. By century's end, the English colonies were ensconced along the Atlantic seaboard—and the foreign population in all the colonies ran to 250,000, placing the native peoples everywhere in danger of annihilation. By the eighteenth century, slaves in Virginia outnumbered whites by three to one. Jamestown slumped into the marsh, a derelict of palisades and wells, streets and sunken brick houses that sat sunrise to sunset awash in rain, light, mosquitoes, and a certain timelessness.

In the 1860s, confederate soldiers planted cannons in a mound of dirt piled on the ruin of Fort James. The island grew so wild in the lees of the Civil War that it was no more than a tangle. Many believed that the fort itself had sunk below the James. And yet, the legends, for ill and good, were beginning to thrive, out beyond the river. An image of Pocahontas was used to sell cigars, and the inherent value of her life had begun its dissipation in commercial exploitation.

America's third President, Thomas Jefferson, sent an

expedition west, under captains Meriwether Lewis and William Clark, to find a passage to the Pacific, the hunt for which had begun here with Smith. Fascinated by the Indians of Virginia and the tragedy of their losses, President Jefferson originally intended to give the Louisiana Purchase, or a lot of it, back to the displaced peoples he so admired. Inspired by his father and his grandfather, who had lived along the James River, President Jefferson carried on some of the fascinations of the early colonials. He pursued a happiness of his own when he allowed his imagination to fill with the stories of Jamestown, to reach empathically out toward others, in whom he and other founding Americans were then drawing strength from the legend of Pocahontas and Smith. The hypocrisy of the founding families' lives is almost unimaginable, but some testament can be made for the implicit hope of multinational unity that was a part of the American dream as Smith captured it for his readers.

In 1631 John Smith lay dying. He was fifty-one, unmarried, and in spite of his exploits in Europe and Tsenacommacoh, he would be remembered for a single sentence or two that he had written in a book. He had tried to revivify for the reader an Indian girl who had saved him once, or maybe twice, and to write of his adventures in a way that was freshly literary—attempting to enjoy a second act in his life. The Indian leaders he wrote about had come to a grief of historic proportion, and the girl he wrote about had died at the height of an unexpected life. Her husband's innovations in tobacco gave rise to a corporate mentality in America that remains at odds with the individual pursuit of self-discovery that she had lived, he had lived—and many others indentured to their times, their lives, and their circumstances. If they outlive their tragedies, it is because they animate certain truths we need to engender who we are. They live on in our imagination. There we, too, may enjoy the pursuits they shared long ago on the overlapping trails of empire—Tsenacommacoh, Virginia, America. ■

EPILOGUE

FOREVER AND EVER YOUR COUNTRYMAN

All Virginia is an estuary. This vast floodplain, watered from mountains west and salted from oceans east, presents a delta whose cycles are fresh. Rivers of the American West, cascading through breach and canyon, declared their exploratory symbolism early, and carried people into the future. Virginia's rivers are smaller and slower, yet they offer a sense of stasis and continuity, and inundate the landscape with history. Virginia is the nation's fountainhead, an invisible aquifer that replenishes with spirit those who search for more than a view in the distance.

As one drives Virginia's country roads, the landscape clicks along in time to the music on the dial. Swamps standing in shadow, a creek knitting grass and reflections, expansive skyline views of western mountains—wherever you look, the past is always present. It is alive in more than the view, as well. From the Blue Ridge to the tidewater, from the capital beltway to the Nascar racetracks, radio towers volley music ranging from the adolescent yearning of oldies to the bitter experience of country across the meteor hills of the Commonwealth. If we see the youth and maturity of a generation in this span, we can also see how that span includes the heroine and the anti-hero of these pages.

What founding families once found so moving that it became their own myth of America has diffused into the moods—and the modes—of national self-perception. In a signal piece of mass entertainment or in acts of foreign imperialism, their old and forgotten dynamic is visible around us daily, it would seem, in the energy of this robust and at times unreflecting nation. We admire independent men and love confident girls, his reckless contempt for authority, her compassion for the poor; and we draw our own respect for individualism from such archetypes. Not a news hour goes by without a bracing story of redemption fashioned around revealing those two imperatives. We see the pursuit of identity in spite of a challenge from the group as a noble cause—a strike against injustice, racism, or any other coercion, even one as tepid as conformity. For those people who look at the story of Pocahontas and John Smith and see only the probable versus the plausible, the factual versus the fanciful, this extra dimension is still fully in play—the way our media present American characters as American Character.

Old towns dogleg throughout Virginia, and in their barrier-reef economy a snazzy new coffee shop opens inside the shell of an old hardware store, and a few doors down an antiques shop has caught hold of the tidal flow of fine furniture. In some respect, these towns fall into an even larger pattern, and if one attains enough altitude, one notices that the alien handprint of eons ago forms an archipelago, a circumference that surrounds a conundrum: a vacancy, a great emptying-out, where the land is not a landscape but an elusive something. The emptiness raises a subtle if disquieting question about American Identity and its health, about whether that emptiness is static or rather a slow-moving dynamic, a new kind of diaspora, one so smoothly encompassing that we cannot gain enough distance to see what is happening.

Any inquiry into this question should entail identity and its reflectors in our landscape. Outside the farming towns and quiet decades in the flickering windshield, you see the new pipeline of our national identity, devoted not to the individual or to the region, the team or the town, but to the brand. Car televisions and radios bombard the mind with corporate messages, and often a child might not escape; even a glance outside might show only the subliminal landscape of capitalism. Today, corporations stream their visual litter around us and remind us that, while the elderly town is a human space of history, the booming new bypass around the town, circumventing the social space of real people, is the exact opposite and points to the future. These four-lane corridors offer a great deal more than access to shopping malls. More comprehensively, they are drive-through virtual malls that extend for miles. They submerge the region, individual, and future below a corporate inundation. Four centuries ago, such total immersion into a corporate destiny became Smith's fight; now for many it is only soothing. The tension between

the individual and the Virginia Company's imperatives are still humming with energy—and urgency, for those who understand.

Our identity starves for nutrients in this time of instant gratification. In our almost seamless disconnect from the landscape, we find ourselves calmed and ordered out of ourselves—an emptiness fed with fast food, anti-depressants, and other false fixes. Into the vacancy within us, companies spill their contents. The economy burgeoning around our new shape—obesity and diabetes in a binge-purge culture, for instance—is an inheritance of Jamestown. We share genes born in starvation, which hoard fat, and a communal memory of hard times. The rugged individualist of Smith has gone into cinema history, and we are the lazy gentlemen of suburbia. The price is still disease, of living beyond our satiety into self-indulgence piqued with corporate malfeasance. If Smith thought he was being fatted for execution, then we may say with certainty that we are, too—for the health-care system awaits us outside the fast-food restaurant in the mall. Our spiritual vacancy, however, cannot be medicated by food, or mitigated by entertainment; we need to reconnect with the landscape, the ineffable surround where identities grow—grounded, literally, with purpose and people and spirit.

The vacancy within seems to mirror the vacancy without—

the continuing stillness of the emptying out, which has prompted us to migrate from the farm to the mall. But if one were to stop next to a cornfield, or a meadow with a game-legged fence hobbling off toward the clouds, one might see the sun strike the land for a bright, transitory instant. And the landscape becomes a palimpsest. Behind the shimmer of an afternoon, the shiver of wind in linden leaves, the faces of an ancient people may appear—silent, eloquent, and necessary.

Virginia is haunted by its past; the things that happened here, and the people they happened to, Native, African, and European, continue to occupy the great stillness of the state—its forest, field, creek, and mountain, its wild places. As a feature of an obsession, ghosts put a human face on the dead. We desire to know them, avert the tragedy, and connect the lines that bind us to them forever and ever as our countrymen. In searching out the past, against the distractions of our day, we seek to hold onto the ineffable even as we see it slipping away under the silt of commercial excess. Perhaps landscape languishes after a tragedy. One neighborhood in Mexico City, where Aztec warriors died to the man defending their capital against the Spanish, remains untainted by success, a consequence that many ascribe to tragedy living on. The same eloquence of stillness can be heard in Virginia today, in battlefield, plantation, floodplain, forest, fen, and great house. Those who died in America's founding holocausts still stand before us in the tenuous shadow of four centuries: Virginia is a land of ghosts. They are the presence one feels coming through the glimmer-field of perception.

Identity is not wholly erasable, however; in spite of their invisibility to so many, and the Racial Integrity Act of 1924, which eliminated them from the state census, Virginia's First People are still very present. Today, the Powhatan may be gone as a distinct set of people by that name, but their gift to us is the near meritocracy of self-sufficiency, which Smith and others

enjoyed. Of the original thirty-two member tribes and other First People of the High Powhatan Era, eight remain: the Upper Mattaponi, the Mattaponi, the Nansemond, the Chickahominy, the Eastern Chickahominy, the Pamunkey, the Rappahannock, and the Monacan. They never left, in spite of the rumors.

The resurgence of Indian nationality is flourishing in a way that is utterly remarkable in its poignancy: an afternoon of eloquence in dance, regalia, language, and song of who they are, where they were, and where they are going. At a powwow, one sees the elegant carriage of the women; the muscular swing of the men's arms, the expression of wind in the swinging fringe of a woman's dress in a grass dance; and the running legs of children who may be as expressive and adorable as the girl known to legend. The powwows are stories in themselves. The speakers always honor the past, and before a powwow begins, the audience is asked to honor the warriors of the various tribes who have fought for the United States. The sense of community, from kids to adults, dance to dinner, among veterans, is unlike any other public event in its power to fashion and to bind a community to its values, its past, and its future. The various styles of regalia recognize tribes and traditions throughout the continent. The unspoken truth is that there in the grassy space, the one that encircles the received and the invented, we witness and participate in identity formation—a renewal set against brilliant mountains.

In the melding of so many elements through ritual, the powwow points us toward a solution to the vast Identity diaspora in the country, but not all of us have the time or inclination to participate—although many find some of these elements in their Sundays in church, or in meditation, or in a New Age evocation of a great spirit without thunder. We live on our own cultural plateau of endless reiterations of the past, presenting us with a diagnosis of cultural exhaustion. How do we address this diaspora, this great emptying out of ourselves, and turn it around in our daily lives?

If I had the answer for that, it would be in the next book; yet, if we cast another look at the Jamestown story, viewing it as a model, we may find some still legible blueprints. The independence in balance with the quest to begin again calls to mind an entrepreneurial vision, one that may be studied and explored in schools, and with a revived examination of the natural example of the Powhatan people. Although we have lost the story of Pocahontas and Smith to entertainment, we can still gain a lot by taking the story back into the class for studies that combine the search for individualism, spirit, community, and self-sufficiency. Children might remember who they are and how to pursue their own happiness—and do so with empathy and respect for spirit and community. Not everyone need be an entrepreneur, but in stories like those of the slave Anthony Johnson and others, the theme of resiliency is instructive. Some immersion into identity-formation in the school curriculum might help fill the inner vacancy with humanity; the alternative is already around us in the form of deleterious corporate content. The past may better direct us.

Among the entrepreneurs who distinguished themselves, Anthony and Mary Johnson offer us a quiet line of Virginia history—the one in which small farmers and entrepreneurs, especially those disenfranchised by race, succeeded, and in time managed to form their own identities against the psychological ruin of captivity and slavery. This story is so complex, though, that to engage the theme with a passion commensurate to its vitality would take many books. But this story, like the one of the Powhatan and the English, is crucial in schools today. The principal people of this story rebelled, every one, against the annihilation of the overlords, and this is the theme of Jamestown that should be their inheritance. Resiliency is the story of identity, not capitulation. While tragedy cannot be forgotten, not every story should be one of despair and loss, for the demoralization of history may further incapacitate the next generation. The remarkable individuals of this story have given us a code for living, one of chance and inordinate strength of heart—examples that may send forth a fresh intelligence for self-reliance.

The architecture of memory stands invisibly in a landscape, and we all revisit the past through stimulation of our senses. The car rolls to a halt; there it is—the childhood house, steeped in shade on a street of sunshine, a place with the first shivers of memory and sentience. What it meant to be, to love, to be loved, to learn and grow—the self's emergence is written inside these panels of light, dark, color, taste and smell—of summer asphalt, of freshly cut grass, the clap of a screen door. From such a point of departure, we fill our minds with stories we need to navigate onward. Tales may be drawn from myth, religion, or gossip, but we fill the space above our minds with figures whose actions reflect the points of light in the sky that we always seem to follow on our migration through the decades. They keep us company; they remind us of who we are and want to be; and they point how far off course we may have traveled. Without a landscape, though, they pale into sentimentality, and vines of creeping neurosis twine round the old framework.

Towns in Virginia stand up like rocks against the pushing current of the faster life elsewhere. The barrier reef stores may thrive along the main street, but many towns anchor themselves with a court square. This feature is at once the communal childhood home for the town, a tribute to memory, and a beacon into the future. The courthouse stands with its Greek revival Doric columns in an echo of antiquity. All round it a green lawn spreads into the shade of great trees. A bronze cannon on wheels may stand there, or a general may sit astride his horse. The sense of place in a court square is static and honorary, the silence devotional. This space is the house of law, and it stands at the ceremonial center of the town. With neighborhoods and years flowing quietly around it, this monument of brick, shade,

and sun reminds us of the continuity of law in a nation of laws. Continuity is what we find again as we roll through the shadowy flickering and remember the self, the one formed inside this prism of meanings, when our senses first opened upon the world, and the architecture of our minds coalesced around the given structures of our lives.

Every year people come to Virginia drawn, perhaps, by a desire to visit historic places as they might a childhood home, to trace the lines of continuity that make this landscape the house of America. Visitors may be compelled by curiosity, piqued by an old romantic story of Pocahontas saving John Smith, or by other legends of founding fathers and battles. The ineluctable connection, though, is that of story and landscape, which becomes an aquifer of emotional memory, and most of all for those who awaken from our collective narcolepsy, troubled by dreams of history.

Those who have awakened have brought history back, vividly. In 1889, two women who were concerned about the swampy island created the Association for the Preservation of Virginia Antiquities, APVA, the first statewide historical association of its kind. Since 1995, APVA archeologists working in Historic Jamestowne have uncovered the fort, long thought to have been lost to the James, and more than one million artifacts that present a more detailed accounting of colonial life, and of a colony more robust than previously thought. Almost a century after the founding of the APVA, the state of Virginia created the Virginia Council On Indians to help garner and steward the revival of Virginia's First People. In Werowocomoco today archeologists and native people, working together, have been finding evidence of how people lived in the Powhatan capital. These associations provide, as do other historic houses, sites, events, and museums, an array of opportunities to rediscover the vital ties that bind us as Americans.

This book is meant to be a gateway book, one that will lead you to the highly detailed and insightful scholarly works that are irresistible reading. (A list of these can be found at the back of this book.) While the scholars' names have not appeared in the text, their research has, though mostly of a factual nature. The errors in romantic sensibility, armchair therapy of the dead, and other amateur inclinations are the misapplied science of this author alone. Although the scholars disagree, their gift to us is an unparalleled discernment into the lives of the foreign and aboriginal people of America, whose cultures go forward into the springs of humanity, and in whose ancient examples we may find ourselves yet again.

The romantic ideas here grew out of an old fascination with what we don't see, but which returns to us. Once upon an academic time, the Parthenon was white because the Greeks so admired stoic severity. Now, paint analysis has shown that it was once as gaudy as a New Orleans cathouse. The same can be said for the Sistine Chapel's ceiling, in whose chiaroscuro Michaelangelo showed the depth of his genius, until restoration removed the candle smoke of centuries and revealed that his taste in color was just as luminous as the cartoons of the "lesser" mannerists who followed him. Between these two examples lies the rubble of Ph.D.s written with absolute certainty.

Was Pocahontas really like the girl and woman described in this book? Was Smith like the man careening dangerously from chapter to chapter? Was Powhatan really a kind of Prospero? There is no way to know. They will remain always mysterious and alluring and tantalizing—even in a relational way, for the statues of Pocahontas and Smith at Historic Jamestowne speak to their acquaintance. His statue stands far above us as a commander— the hero he always wanted to be—but hers stands at ground level, as a person. He stares out at the world; she opens her hands at her side, in personal welcome. Neither statue addresses the other but they relate across some eighty yards, indirectly. Their faces of bronze, cool and impassive, stare across the James and into unimaginable ages. In four centuries beyond the sunrise, after the United States has vanished or morphed beyond recognition, perhaps the island and their statues will slip under the slow apocalypse of a rising ocean.

Although we cannot know the people who populate this story of Jamestown, perhaps the journals present information that does relate them in terms that we may transpose into our own, just as we would transpose the anachronisms of the journals. If we leave aside for a moment the question of how much history is fiction and how much fantasy, then we can say that the phantasmagoria of their lives is animated by the unknown motivations of the human heart in conflict with itself. The journals and histories of the time offer us the frustrations of a dream, its clarity and blurriness. Nothing would be less surprising than to learn that their lives were less smoky and more colorful than anything we now believe. The people you have read about in these pages are with us, in their confusion and desire, aspiration and disquiet, in the way we choose to remember them—and to honor their haunting.

Where to from here is the endless question in all our searching, and though you already know this, no story ends where you think it will.

ACKNOWLEDGEMENTS

ACTORS: In the style of film credits, we would like to thank, first, the actors who played the leading roles in this book.

To portray native people in this book, we felt it was our moral obligation to ask descendants of the Powhatan and other Virginia Indian tribes to portray their ancestors. Those who played the famous brought history and authenticity.

Three Chickahominy young women portrayed Pocahontas, from ages nine to nineteen. Sierra Adkins brought a sparkling intelligence and vivacity to her role as the young Pocahontas. Rachel Stewart gave a lively presence to our middle Pocahontas. And Jessica Canaday endowed the older Pocahontas with resolve, authority and tragedy.

Our John Smith could not have been played better than he was by Ryan Norton, who died in a motorcycle accident not long after working on this book. Ryan left us one and all with a powerful impression of his youth and tenacity—qualities that he brought to his portrayal of Smith, and which make him unforgettable in these pages. He died on May 14th at the age of 29, the same day the English wanted to hang John Smith, then 29.

Jerry Fortune (Rappahannock) created our robust Powhatan, and Austin Two Feathers (Notoweega) created Opechancanough and Uttamakkomin with equal conviction, and more than this, volunteered regalia, tools, weapons, and equipment that were centerpieces in many shots.

Dick Cheatham, a descendant of John Rolfe, brought his personal knowledge and bearing on his ancestor to making his portrayal live.

Dennis Strawderman gave Christopher Newport a perfect bearing, and brought a group of volunteers, the Henricus Militia, to help portray the English in battle.

Didier Occident and Sherri Glover gave Anthony and Mary Johnson poignant life.

SPONSORS: No book like this one could have been made without the life-giving help of a team of great sponsors. The Dominion team, with Eva Teig Hardy, Marjorie Greer, and William Hall, were wonderful and steadfast. Robert H. Smith was more than a mentor, and his momentum helped us to carry on round the seasons. We cannot quite ever thank Jeanne J. Miller and Patrick J. Dexter for their early and enthusiastic corporate support at ExxonMobil, which Allison Leo Rana carried on. The Virginia Foundation for the Humanities was instrumental in its support of photographic expeditions and in compensating the various scholars who vetted the text, and we thank Robert Vaughan and David Bearinger. For the Virginia National Bank, Mark Giles was, as always, a mentor and helped not only with support, but also with wisdom and coaching that we could not have done without. We also thank Embarq, which was assisted by Margaret Wright. Henry Doggett kindly provided us with road maps of state politics. Susan Magill was a boon, and we cannot thank her enough for her sponsorship help and in receiving U.S. Senator John Warner's endorsement. We also thank Senator George Allen for his kind endorsement.

We are delighted to thank Bruce and Jim Murray for their help with vital phases in the book's early development. We also thank Charles Euchner for his fund-raising expertise, along with Susan Payne, and Sheldon Bernstein, for their crucial ideas. Advice from Charlie Selheimer, Ben Dendy, Frank Atkinson, Eliza O'Connell, and Kathryn Carr was very helpful. And Nelson Lankford and Charles Bryan at the Virginia Historical Society were more than helpful.

Simply put, this mission to bring history to life for the 400th anniversary of Jamestown, in 2007, and to reawaken national empathies, could not have been undertaken without their generosity of mind and spirit. And to them, we owe them our deeply felt thanks

RIVANNA FOUNDATION: Assistance and advice with the Rivanna Foundation came from Mac Thompson, Brock Green, and Paul Wagner. Without the tireless work of Richard Howard-Smith, we simply could not have done anything, period. Their help in the exhausting labyrinth of legal code was crucial, and we thank them for all their hours and help.

EDITORIAL: This book about Jamestown could not have been written smoothly without expert editorial advice and help. Barbara Brownell Grogan came on board first with crucial advice, heart, and guidance, followed by Katie Kroloff, who read the evolving script, and was always insightful and encouraging during the winter of composition. Jane Sunderland came in with a fine eye to structure and chronology. Susan Poole checked the facts, and Rebecca Barns did the final read-through. These brilliant women stood present, spoke with clarity and conviction, and the impossible got done. Without them, the text would be less than it is, and I owe them all thanks for its final realization as a work. And we want to thank former Virginia Governor Mark Warner for his wonderful introduction, and Grant Neely for his thoughtful editorial contribution.

ADVICE AND SCHOLARS: We would have been lost had we not encountered many wonderful people along the way, who offered advice and insight into the story. Mary Maynor (Lumbee) shared historical and present-day Indian culture. One of my most important advisors was Karenne Wood (Monacan), chair of the Virginia Council on Indians, who not only engaged me in many conversations, but also read and vetted the manuscript in several drafts. Author and professor at William & Mary, Martin Gallivan, also vetted the text and helped me out of error and confusion. Their scholarly insights were more than considerate—they helped make the text viable.

Many people of English and Indian ancestry came forward with so many tales and opinions, that you could see how alive the Jamestown story still is. I would be remiss if I did not confess to a beginner's step in anthropology—of having lost my heart to the new culture. The Virginia Indian community took me in, and through their powwows, friendship, conversation, and challenges, community and feeling, they helped me find a way into the story. I want to thank Maria Holland (Taino), David Perry (Tuscarora), and Dana Adkins (Chickahominy) for their insights, observations, and personal stories. Other stories that were helpful and inspiring came from Wendy Summer, and Pearl Bobo.

CASTING: We went to many powwows in search of people to play parts in the book, and Debby Moore (Pamunkey) was very helpful with our search, as was Kay Oxendine (Haliwa-Saponi). Chickahominy Chief Steve Adkins and Assistant Chief, Wayne Adkins, gave us a robust welcome to their community that proved crucial in casting the book. Additional casting help came from Keith Wynn, Powwow Coordinator, of the Chickahominy tribe. Elizabeth Hupert (Eastern Band Cherokee) assisted us in reaching the many others who later participated in the photographs. Other people who helped with casting include Judith Fortune (Rappahannock) and Faye Fortune (Rappahannock).

LOCATIONS: Ernest Skinner gave us vital help in finding locations, in casting the book, and in creating scenes, whether working around his film crew or independently with his actors. Homer Lanier of Jamestown Settlement was often cheerfully instructive, and kept everything happening, while Eric Speth, the captain of the recreated Susan Constant steered us safely home one stormy day. We thank him, along with Jack Fisk, and Bill Kelso in Historic Jamestowne and the APVA,

for their insights. Deborah Padgett of the Jamestown Settlement offered us great access to the James Fort and the Powhatan Indian village. Jamie Jameson at Berkeley Plantation also made us welcome with his time and landscape as photography locations. Captain Mike Minarik took us down the Chickahominy and James, so we could feel some of the wilderness. Mike Litterest helped us with Jamestown National Park. Furlong Baldwin guided us round his grounds and family history one fine day on the Eastern shore. Pete McKee helped us with location photography and costumes at Henricus Historical Park. Sue Wilkerson, St. Mary's City, MD helped us get aboard the *Dove*. Rita McClenny and Andy Edmunds of the Virginia Film Office assisted us. And thanks go also to the Blackfriars Playhouse, Staunton, VA, for allowing us to photograph their performance of *The Tempest*.

MAKEUP and WARDROBE: The photographs would not have hit their mark without the help of various assistants on every shoot. Brenda Rousseau, the costume designer, helped us bring the past alive. Jarod Jefferies, of London Hair Design, gave our players their authentic appearances. Historical costume expert, Charlene Bullard and makeup artist, Sharon Barrett gave hair, makeup, and clothing their polished appearance.

PHOTOGRAPHY: Creative assistance in photography production came from Emily P. Taylor. She was instrumental in coordinating all the phases that include casting, locations, regalia, costumes, makeup, troubleshooting, and the difficult turns of making this book. Aerial photographs were created with the expert help of pilot Gary Livack. Other photography assistants were Adam Litvin and Luca Dicecco. David DesRoches also helped on a big shooting day. Help with photos and computers came from Jon Golden.

NATIVE AMERICAN ACTORS: Austin Lee Bess, Blake Bess, Yuri Cherepnya, Mark and Christian Castonguay, David Perry (Tuscarora), Rose Powhatan (Pamunkey); Courtney Wynn (Chickahominy); Keith Anderson (Catawba/Lumbee); Preston Adkins, (Chickahominy); Kirk Moore (Pamunkey); Crystal, Carmen, and Tahlia Wynn (Chickahominy); Leahmarie Gottlieb; Tammie Taylor; Gigi Almacher; Khrys Vaughan; Teddy Wood; Eloise Brunic (Cherokee); Cyril Taylor; Robert Narcomey; Shannon Holden; Ashton Chaske; Ethan Hotain; Dakota; Dona, Maya, and Melinda Richardson (Meherrin); Dan Grogan (Paleo Man)

ENGLISH ACTORS: Dusty Simmons; Bradley Jenkins; Matt Jenkins, Stephen Sent, Lowell Coleman, Terry Bond, Cynthia Daniel, Mary Strawderman, Duane Baldwin, Ronald Blackburn, Lindsay Gray, Calvin Jenkins, Jennifer Hogg, Brenden Preddy, Alena Preddy, Jack Oblein, Michael Hickory, Michael Fitts, Bryan Cox, Benjamin Roesler, S. Preston Duncan; Susan Heyward as Miranda; Matthew Sincell as Ferdinand; and David Loar as Prospero

CREW OF THE SUSAN CONSTANT: Eric Speth, Captain. Todd Egnor, Whit Perry, Kaia Danyluk, Homer Lanier, Mike Lund, Mike Crookshank, Jaie Pizzetti, James Harrison, Jim Dillard, Adam Frisch, Richard Gibson, Susan Harris, Gary Harvey, Paul Huber, Douglas Lindeman, Stelphen Link, Ronald Lippert, Frank Mcguirk, Chuck Moody, Gary Ogden, Jenna Ogden, Geoff Perkins, Ian Perkins, Dylan Perry, Terry Robertson, John Robinson, Catherine Schiavone, Martin Sekula, Frederick Siegel, Robert Smith, Warren Speth, Noel Veden and Richard Watkins. ∎

BIBLIOGRAPHY

Mossiker, Frances (1996), *Pocahontas: The Life and Legend* New York: Da Capo Press

Lemay, J.A. Leo (1992), *Did Pocahontas Save Captain John Smith?* The University of Georgia Press, Athens and London

Gladwell, Malcolm (2005), *Blink: The Power of Thinking Without Thinking* Little, Brown and Company, New York and Boston

Robinson, Jr., W. Stitt (1957) *Mother Earth: Land Grants in Virginia, 1607-1699* The Virginia 350th Anniversary Celebration Corporation MCMLVII

Poag, C. Wylie (1999) *Chesapeake Invader: Discovering America's Giant Meteorite Crater* Princeton University Press, Princeton, New Jersey

Gleach, Frederick W. (1997) *Powhatan's World and Colonial Virginia: A Conflict of Cultures* The University of Nebraska Press, Lincoln and London

Horn, James (2005) *A Land as God Made It: Jamestown and the Birth of America* Basic Books, New York

Horn, James (1994) *Adapting to a New World: English Society in the Seventeenth-Century Chesapeake* University of North Carolina Press Chapel Hill and London

Bloom, Harold (1998) *Shakespeare: The Invention of the Human* Riverhead Books, New York

Barnett, Sylvan, Ed. (1963) *The Complete Signet Classic Shakespeare* Harcourt, Brace, Jovanovich New York, Chicago, San Francisco, Atlanta

Isaac, Rhys (1982) *The Transformation of Virginia 1740-1790* University of North Carolina Press Chapel Hill and London

Jackson, John Brinckerhoff (1994) *A Sense of Place, A Sense of Time* Yale University Press New Haven and London

Sullivan, George (2002) *Pocahontas* Scholastic Reference

Cosgrove, Denis E. (1984) *Social Formation and Symbolic Landscape* University of Wisconsin Press Madison and London

De Tocqueville, Alexis, Mayer, J.P. Ed. (1969) *Democracy in America* Harper & Row New York

Diamond, Jared (1999) *Guns, Germs, and Steel: The Fates of Human Societies* W.W. Norton & Company New York and London

Schama, Simon (1995) *Landscape and Memory* Alfred A. Knopf New York

Gladwell, Malcolm (2000) *The Tipping Point: How Little Things Can Make a Big Difference* Little, Brown and Company Boston, New York, London

Wright, Jr., J. Leitch (1981) *The Only Land They Knew: American Indians in the Old South* University of Nebraska Press Lincoln and London

Townsend, Camilla (2004) *Pocahontas and the Powhatan Dilemma* Hill and Wang New York

Haile, Edward Wright, Ed. (1998) *Jamestown Narratives: Eyewitness Accounts of the Virginia Colony, The First Decade: 1607-1617* RoundHouse Champlain, Virginia

Kupperman, Karen Ordahl, Ed. (1988) *Captain John Smith: A Select Edition of his Writings* University of North Carolina Press Chapel Hill & London

Breen, T.H., & Innes, Stephen (1980) *"Myne Owne Ground" : Race and Freedom on Virginia's Eastern Shore, 1640-1676* Oxford University Press New York, Oxford

Dabney, Virginius (1971) *Virginia, The New Dominion: A History from 1607 to the Present* University of Virginia Press Charlottesville

Gallivan, Martin D. (2003) *James River Chiefdoms: The Rise of Social Inequality in the Chesapeake* University of Nebraska Press Lincoln and London

Allen, Paula Gunn (2003) *Pocahontas: Medicine Woman, Spy, Entrepreneur, Diplomat* HarperCollins New York

Rountree, Helen C. (2005) *Pocahontas, Powhatan, Opechancanough: Three Indian Lives Changed by Jamestown* University of Virginia Press Charlottesville and London

Rountree, Helen C. (1990) *Pocahontas's People: The Powhatan Indians of Virginia Through Four Centuries* University of Oklahoma Press Norman and London

Armstrong, Karen (1993) *A History of God: The 4000-Year Quest of Judaism, Christianity and Islam* Ballantine Books, New York

Lasch, Christopher (1979) *The Culture of Narcissism: American Life in an Age of Diminishing Expectations* W.W. Norton & Company New York London

Mann, Charles C. (2005) *1491: New Revelations of the Americas Before Columbus* Alfred A. Knopf New York

Cooke, Alistair (1973) *Alistair Cooke's America* Alfred A. Knopf New York

Reinhart, Theodore R., Hodges, Mary Ellen, Eds. (1991) *Late Archaic and Early Woodland Research in Virginia: A Synthesis.* Special Publication No. 23 of the Archeological Society of Virginia

Reinhart, Theodore R., Hodges, Mary Ellen, Eds (1992) *Middle and Late Woodland Research in Virginia: A Synthesis Special Publication No. 29* of the Archeological Society of Virginia

Reinhart, Theodore R., Hodges, Mary Ellen, Eds (1990) *Early and Middle Archaic Research in Virginia: A Synthesis* Special Publication No. 22 of the Archeological Society of Virginia

Wittkofski, J. Mark and Theodore R. Reinhart, Eds. (1989) *Paleoindian Research in Virginia: A Synthesis Special Publication No. 19* of the Archeological Society of Virginia

Gleach, Frederich W., *Pocahontas: An Exercise in Mythmaking and Marketing. New Perspectives on North America: cultures, histories, and representations* Sergei A. Kan and Pauline Turner Strong, eds. University of Nebraska Press, 2006

Hantman, Jeffrey L., *Caliban's Own Voice: American Indian Views of the Other in Colonial Virginia New Literary History*, 1992

DSM-IV - Diagnostic and Statisical Manual of Mental Disorders, Fourth Edition, American Pyschiatric Association

EMPIRES IN THE FOREST
Jamestown and the Beginning of America

Copyright 2006 Rivanna Foundation

Text Copyright 2006 Avery Chenoweth

Photography Copyright 2006 Robert Llewellyn

Published by Rivanna Foundation
885 Reas Ford Road, Earlysville, Virginia   22936
434.973.8000

Distributed by University of Virginia Press
Charlottesville and London
www.upress.virginia.edu

Book Design by Michael Fitts

Production Assistant, Photography: Emily P. Taylor

Printed and bound in Canada

First Edition

Library of Congress Cataloging-in-Publication Data

Chenoweth, Avery.
Empires in the Forest: Jamestown and the Beginning of America / words, Avery Chenoweth; photographs, Robert Llewellyn.—1st ed.

ISBN 0-9742707-0-9
1. Jamestown—History. 2. Pocahontas—biography 3. John Smith—biography 4. Chief Powhatan—biography 5. Landscape—Virginia—Henricus—History 6. Opechancanough—history, biography 7. John Rolfe—tobacco 8. Indians of North America—Virginia Tribes—Starving Time—*The Tempest*—Bacon's Rebellion—Pocahontas kidnapping—Christopher Newport—History. 9. Llewellyn, Robert—photographs 10. Chenoweth, Avery—history, biography

Library of Congress Control Number: 2006931172